DO NOT TEST US

One Man's Ventures into the Psychic World

Statement by the Author

This book is nonfiction. I have simply recorded psychic events that have occurred to me and to people I know. Many of these friends have given me permission to use their real names, which I have not done because they might later change their minds. Also, I wish to protect their privacy.

To those of you who are well-read on the subject, I have no particular advice. To those of you who are novices, let me say that I sincerely hope this book will pique your curiosity and you will read more and explore further—but please keep in mind that it is imperative for you to keep one foot on the ground. You will see why.

Though much in these pages will seem weird and hard to accept, I hope, and believe, they will hold your attention.

Dick Walker

9-23-90

TO HARRY + SHEILA

WITH VERY BEST WISHES

Dan Warren

DO NOT TEST US

One Man's Ventures into the Psychic World

By
Dick Walker

Binford & Mort

Thomas Binford, Publisher

2536 S.E. Eleventh • Portland, Oregon 97202

I dedicate this book to my father, Raymond B. Walker, who "graduated with honors" not long ago. Even though we are no longer in the same state of consciousness, I frequently feel his loving presence, and I strongly suspect that he is aware of this book.

Printed in the United States of America
Library of Congress Catalog Card Number: 78-57020
ISBN: 0-8323-0307-0
First Edition 1978

Contents

Introduction

My interest in psychic phenomena goes back a long, long way. My father was a prominent Congregational minister in downtown Portland, Oregon, and in his study he had a huge library. One day when I was looking over the shelves, I noticed the title, *Nothing So Strange*, a book written by Margueritt Bro. Dad said, "Take it home and read it. You'll find it fascinating."

I read this book and I was not only fascinated, I was hooked. It was the biography of Arthur Ford, one of the world's greatest psychics. Ford would go into a trance, and the voices of persons who had died years before could be heard through his vocal cords. It appeared he could slip into another dimension or state of consciousness, and actually communicate with people long deceased.

I soon discovered that many books had been written on the subject of psychic phenomena by reputable researchers such as, Sir Oliver Lodge, the great British physicist; Dr. Charles Richet, noted French psychical researcher and winner of the Nobel prize in physiology; and Dr. Alfred Russel Wallace, co-discoverer with Darwin of the theory of natural selection. To my astonishment, I learned that these scientists openly practiced and endorsed spiritualism. Other world-famous persons who regularly allegedly communicated with the dead through mediums include Abraham Lincoln, Thomas Edison, and Sir Arthur Conan Doyle.

My mother, who for reasons unknown to me, was singularly opposed to all things pertaining to metaphysics, once said, "Son, only an ignoramus has anything to do with the occult— please stay away from it!" I decided not to heed her advice and became an "ignoramus" who read every book I could find on psychical research, attended lectures, enrolled in college classes on parapsychology, and investigated seance-room phenomena.

Occasionally, I was confronted with other firm verbal opposition to my search for occult knowledge. An example follows:

"But, Mr. Walker, you should accept the authority of the Bible, which, of course, is the truth. In return for your trust, you will receive peace, security, salvation, and you most certainly will not have to explore in the devil's backyard, which you are now doing."

"Well, sir, your philosophy may be right for you. You are equating religious authority with truth and you believe there is no need to try to solve the mysteries of life, death, creation, and so on. I envy the comfort your faith gives you. I suppose I should be enjoying the same comfort because of the many years I lived in the parsonage with my parents. However, for some reason, faith didn't take, and I felt a great need for proof. When I found that anyone could explore the field of psychic phenomena, I enthusiastically jumped in with both feet. The results of my research, although often mind-boggling, have been comforting to a degree and I think I have grown a little."

"Perhaps, Mr. Walker, but how you can get any comfort from the devil is something I don't understand."

And I certainly do not understand the mysterious laws which govern E.S.P., clairvoyance, miraculous healings, materializations and apparent communication with those beyond the grave. I do believe, however, that the search for this knowledge does not in any way conflict with religious principles. Long ago, a much-quoted gentleman said, "If we don't knock, the door will remain closed."

1

My First Seance

I was intensely curious about the world of psychic phenomena, and eager to investigate it. The opportunity arrived through a family friend, a former Portland police chief. One of his jobs had been to investigate and arrest fraudulent fortune tellers and mediums. He reported that eighty percent were frauds but twenty percent had proved genuine. That twenty percent was what I wanted to find out about. The Chief made it possible.

"If you would like to explore this subject further, Dick, I'll give you the name and telephone number of a man who lives in _____." He mentioned a small town in Oregon, about seventy-five miles from Portland.

"This man and his wife are spiritualists," the Chief told me. "He is a true sensitive and he produces genuine phenomena. Call him and ask him if you can attend one of their sittings. There will be no charge, and you will be served ice cream and cake after the meeting."

No charge and free food! How could I lose other than a few gallons of gas?

So I telephoned. A soft voice answered, "The Chief asked you to call? Fine! We have room for nine people. You will be most welcome, and you may bring your wife or a friend. If you bring someone with you next Tuesday night, there will be seven guests at the sitting. We will start at eight o'clock and the session will last about two hours."

When I told my wife, Dorothy, that we were going to a seance, she looked at me bleakly and asked, "Do I have to go?"

"Well, no," I replied, "but it's supposed to be legitimate. It should be an interesting experience."

Dorothy is one of those persons who have definite psychic qualities. Occasionally, we would engage in parlor games with friends, such as playing the Ouija board and tipping the table.*

When Dorothy placed her hands on the table, it would immediately shake violently. Or if a couple were getting very little movement on the Ouija Board—to be discussed in a later chapter—one of them would call, "Hey, Dorothy, come over and take my place. We want to see some action." And action they would get! As soon as her fingers rested on the planchette, it started moving rapidly across the board.

Her mother and grandmother also had psychic qualities, as does our daughter. Psychic research has found that these qualities are indeed inherited. With study, most people who

---

*Table tipping was started over a century ago by family groups attempting to communicate with the spirit world. Today, more as a social game, several people sit around a table with their hands flat on the surface, fingers touching. After a few minutes the fingers start to tingle, which indicates that action is about to start. Suddenly the table starts to shake sideways, slowly at first, and then the tempo increases. Questions are asked and the table taps its legs once for no and twice for yes. Frequently the table will rise completely off the floor and remain suspended in the air for several seconds. Some researchers believe that the table movement is due to unconscious muscular action on the part of the sitters. To date, however, most investigators offer no explanation for the levitation of the table.

have them could become excellent sensitives or mediums, yet most who start to develop these abilities become apprehensive and abandon their study.

Anyway, when the appointed Tuesday evening arrived, Dorothy decided to go along. We were cordially greeted at the door by our host, Mr. Reiner, a pleasant middle-aged man who introduced us to his wife and the five other guests with whom we were to sit.

We were then ushered into another room, approximately twelve by twelve feet, with nine chairs spaced out around the walls. A blanket securely covered the one window so absolutely no light could get into the room from the outside. The walls were covered with oil paintings of faces of men and women of various nationalities. There was nothing particularly unusual about these pictures except the eyes, which were so lifelike they seemed to follow our every movement.

Our host said that the pictures had been painted by a sensitive when in a trance and that all these people had actually lived many years ago. He added that some of them would be visiting us that evening from the spirit world and would be playing the toy musical instruments that were spread over the floor.

One picture was of a dignified Chinese gentleman by the name of Dr. Chin. He was to be the moderator of the sitting that evening. He would come in first and would leave last. He would also help to prevent any undesirable spirits from joining the meeting.

When our host gave us this information, it was difficult not to smile. My reason told me that nothing like this could possibly happen. Still, I had had one small jolt, from the eyes in those paintings. They were astounding, and everyone in attendance agreed that the eyes certainly appeared to be alive.

We stood there looking around the room. On the floor were a dozen or more toy musical instruments including a xylophone which later would wind up on my lap. There were also several pads of blank paper and pencils and two aluminum trumpets. The trumpets, which resembled dunce caps, were made in three sections and when extended were about three feet long. Mr. Reiner said their purpose was to amplify the voices of the spirits. Each trumpet had a luminous band around the widest section.

Our host stated that the spirits would play the toy musical instruments, would write the names of our individual spirit guides on the paper, and would whisper messages to us through the trumpets. He further explained that at the end of the sitting, the spirits would pull the trumpet sections apart and scatter them over the floor. He saw the smile which I tried to conceal and added, "We are not asking you to believe our explanation for the phenomena you're going to experience. However, we hope you will keep an open mind and not ridicule us."

Fair enough, I thought, wishing he had not seen my disbelieving smile.

"Where do we sit?" I asked.

"Anywhere you wish," he replied. I chose the chair next to him; and, of course, Dorothy, who I could see was uneasy, sat next to me. Mr. Reiner turned out the lights. All we could see, in the pitch blackness, were the two luminous bands around the trumpets.

"Why does it have to be so dark?" I asked.

"It seems that darkness is as necessary for the production of spirit manifestations as it is to the germination of plant and animal life. We have been told by the spirits that a form of electricity, not yet discovered by our earth-plane scientists, enables them to visit us briefly under certain conditions. Like the radio, their reception is much better at night. I am aware that you are very skeptical and perhaps a bit apprehensive at this stage of your exploration. You are thinking that this

My First Seance 5

darkness might conceal the practice of fraud. Rest assured, this is not the case. Furthermore, no one has ever been injured at a seance except the medium."

"Do we have to be quiet and should we hold hands?" someone asked.

"Not at all necessary," Reiner replied, "although we can take hands when our spirit guests arrive, so you will know that no one has left his chair. And now, if everyone will please recite the Lord's Prayer. . . ." This we did, and it was followed by a prayer from Mr. Reiner, in which he asked that a protective white light encompass our circle, preventing any bad entities from joining us.

After this, we all chatted for about fifteen minutes, until our host suddenly said, "Welcome, Dr. Chin. Dr. Chin is now with us. Soon there will be much activity." Before he had finished speaking, the two trumpets left the floor with incredible speed and flew from side to side of the room at near ceiling height. Of course the trumpets themselves were not visible in the darkened room, but we could see the luminous bands around them.

This is quite a trick, I thought. I must find out how it is done.

Suddenly all the toy instruments were being played and the drums, tambourines, mouth organs, flutes, music boxes and horns made a bedlam of noise. The xylophone had been dropped in my lap and someone was striking the keys vigorously and inharmoniously.

To find out who these tricksters were that were making all this racket, I spoke up, requesting that all should speak out from their chairs and hold hands with their neighbors. I reached out for my wife's hand and Mr. Reiner's, who was seated next to me. Since everyone cooperated, I had to conclude that all were in their chairs.

There was only one other answer that I could think of:
several people must have entered the room in the
dark—through a trapdoor, maybe—and were now blowing
the horns and making this tremendous disturbance with the
toy instruments.

Releasing my grip on Mr. Reiner's hand, I asked, "Where is
the trapdoor?"

"We don't engage in trickery here, Mr. Walker."

The activity accelerated. All around the circle, people were
exclaiming.

"Someone is stroking my hair!"

"I think a trumpet is tapping my knee!" And so on.

Dorothy nervously said, "Something is flipping my beads
around my neck!"

I saw the luminous band around a trumpet near the ceiling
streak toward my head. Then I felt the cold metal of the
trumpet on my cheek, stroking gently.

Remarkable, I thought. Whoever was producing this
chicanery had to be wearing some kind of infrared glasses in
order to see in the dark. Then I had another thought: There
must be elaborate equipment here, to produce these phenomena. But why? There was no admission charge, and no zealous
missionary work was being done to interest us in spiritualism.

Some of the sitters in the room, including my wife, were
becoming increasingly vocal about being touched by the so-
called spirits. Mr. Reiner said, "You are being stroked and
caressed by loved ones who are no longer on this plane. If this
disturbs you, ask them to stop and they will, immediately. Or
you can will them to stop without speaking."

Aha! I thought. Mr. Reiner had made his first mistake—
asking them to stop without speaking. The stroking of the
trumpet had moved from my cheek to my hair. First, in a
loud voice, I commanded "Stop!" Instantly the stroking stop-

ped. Then I said, "You may start again." The caressing started again.

Now, I said to myself, I'll really catch them. I mentally said, Stop! The stroking stopped.

Start! I mentally commanded. It started again. Over and over, I gave these mental commands and each time they were obeyed. Others in the room were also experimenting with the mental commands, and they were having the same results. I could hear somebody's puzzled voice asking, "Do they stop for you, too?" This was really bewildering.

Well, there was only one explanation, I thought at last. Someone in this room was a mind reader, and it was very likely Mr. Reiner himself. Mind reading must be remarkable, but has science actually proved it to be a fact? I didn't know. The complacency I had brought to the meeting was weakening. Later, it was going to be completely demolished.

I asked Mr. Reiner, "Can you see the spirits in the room now?"

"Some of them," he replied. "For example, there's a man standing behind you and I will describe him to you." He accurately described a very close friend who had died several months previously: the small scar on his cheek, the gold cap on a tooth, the receding hairline, the blue-gray eyes, the elfish smile, the muscular body structure, and the clothes he was wearing the day he died.

Then Reiner said, "Only you and his wife called him by a nickname his mother had given him. I can't quite get it. Wait. It's something like Blinky. No, Pinky. No, that's wrong, too. I've got it...Chinky!" Now the chills were going up and down my spine. This was a hit. The name we called him was indeed Chinky.

Reiner then said, "Some of our sitters may see a yellow light where he's standing."

Dorothy exclaimed, "I wondered what that light was doing there!" From across the room another said, "I was going to ask about that yellow light." Of course I turned around but I could see nothing. Nor did the other sitters see a light.

I have read that we all have inborn psychic abilities and that in some people these are more developed than in others. Apparently, my wife and the other sitter who witnessed the light were more psychic than the rest that evening—with the exception, of course, of Mr. Reiner. At that time I considered Mr. Reiner to be a master magician and mind reader. . . .

The luminous bands on the two trumpets were now stationary in the middle of the room, about four feet in the air, and my head was being stroked by something else. Most of the other sitters had asked, audibly, not to be touched. The tone of their voices indicated nervousness; a couple were clearly frightened. I was excited but not frightened. I was enormously curious and determined, somehow, to get to the bottom of all this.

Mr. Reiner, sitting next to me, suddenly called out," Ssh, listen to the trumpet." Soon we began to hear faint whispers coming from one of the trumpets. We strained our ears. "Chinky, Chinky, Chinky," came through. The rest of the words we couldn't get. I asked Mr. Reiner if he could understand them.

"Something about Stanley and John Bennett," he said. "I didn't get the rest." Now, this was very interesting to me. Chinky and I had taken voice lessons from John Bennett, and John Bennett taught the Stanley Method of voice development.

The whispering from the trumpet ceased. Again the luminous bands of both trumpets flew around the room so fast that our eyes could scarcely follow them—and the toy musical instruments resumed their bedlam of discordant sounds.

"Why all this inharmonious noise?" I asked Mr. Reiner.

"It's very difficult for these spirits to get into our earth plane," he said, "and they want to attract our attention. Some of them are juvenile and immature and some are very intellectual. There are also relatives and friends of people who are sitting with us tonight, and they desperately want to make themselves known." This explanation didn't satisfy me, but I pressed him no further at the time.

Another half hour of noise ensued with the trumpets again producing whispers that no one could understand. Soon our host announced:

"Each of you will receive a piece of paper upon which will be the name of his or her spirit guide." There was silence, followed by exclamations: "I can hear the rustling of paper by my head," "I've been given a piece of paper," "There's a paper in my lap," and so forth.

It seemed to me that several people had to be out of their chairs making these noises. Again I asked everyone to identify himself and noted the direction of the sound of the voice. All appeared to be in their chairs. Then it occurred to me that some kind of apparatus must be coming down from the ceiling or up through the floor. Perhaps I could check this out when the sitting was over. . . .

Now the trumpet began to whisper again. Because Mr. and Mrs. Reiner seemed to hear its words better than the rest of us, they acted as interpreters.

"Did I hear my name then?" one of the sitters asked.

"Yes," replied Mrs. Reiner. "It's your mother and she said this is not a good time to sell your house. I couldn't understand the rest of her message."

"We just couldn't make up our minds if we should sell now," the sitter commented.

Several messages came through for other sitters, but no more came for me. Soon Reiner announced, "Dr. Chin says he has to leave now and wishes you all a safe journey back to your homes. Will you please recite with me the Twenty-Third Psalm."

During the last ten minutes the noise had been subsiding. After a weak plink on a key, the xylophone left my lap and the trumpet sections fell to the floor with a crash. Then all was silent. Mr. Reiner turned on the light. The trumpets had been pulled apart and their sections were scattered over the floor among the toy instruments, pads and pencils. Each one in the circle held a piece of paper in his hand, upon which was printed the name of his spirit guide. Mine was Kado Dos.

"Where did Kado Dos live?" I asked my host.

"I believe the spirits said in Samoa," replied Mr. Reiner.

Let me interpolate, right here, an interesting little follow-up to this name of Kado Dos. Several months after this first sitting, Dorothy and I were serving as social directors on a cruise ship going to Australia. One of our ports of call was Pago Pago, Samoa. When we landed there, I went into the post office and asked the postmaster if he had ever heard the name Kado Dos. He answered, "Yes, there used to be a man by that name who lived on the other side of the island, near where Robert Louis Stevenson is buried. I believe he and his family are all dead now."

Back to our first sitting. . . . We all went into the living room for a discussion session while Mrs. Reiner prepared dessert. "Then you are not a trance medium?" someone asked Mr. Reiner.

"No," he replied. "I never lose consciousness. When conditions are right I can see people who are no longer on our earth plane, and I always see Dr. Chin when he arrives. He is a distinguished-looking, elderly Chinese gentleman who wears a long white robe. At times I can also hear spirits talk, though usually with difficulty. I don't hear them, audibly, unless it's through the trumpet, but I do occasionally hear their voices in my head."

"When did you first realize you were psychic?"

"I was brought up in a small town in the East," he said. "When I was about seven or eight years old, several of us boys would visit a very old haunted house. We could all hear footsteps and doors slammed. However, I was the only one who could see who was making these noises. They were men and women who wore funny-looking clothes—that's what I called them then. Now, of course, I realize they were wearing old-fashioned clothes."

Mrs. Reiner interrupted with the ice cream, cake and cookies. I asked if I could make a contribution to help defray the expenses of the dessert, but she would not hear of it: "I should say not! You are our guests and we are delighted to have you with us."

Two of the other guests were noticeably shaken by this experience in the dark. It was their first sitting, as it was ours. One of them was the principal of an elementary school in the area; the other was his wife, a grade-school teacher. The other three guests that evening were long-time spiritualists—a building contractor and his wife, and a bus driver who was not married.

It was getting late, and we had a long drive ahead of us in the pouring rain, so it was time to leave. I asked Mr. Reiner if we could return next week and sit again.

"You will be most welcome," he said. "But you may not wish to return because there is a strong possibility that you will have visitors before you go to sleep tonight. This greatly disturbs some people, even though they have nothing to fear."

"I don't understand what you mean, Mr. Reiner."

"Well, I know it may sound ridiculous to those who are not knowledgeable about spiritualism, but it seems that usually, after the first sitting, spirits follow you home. They try, and usually succeed, in making themselves known."

At this remark I couldn't repress a smile. I tried to make it cordial rather than disbelieving and I said, "Thanks for the warning. We'll keep a sharp lookout for spirits."

This was too much, I thought, spirits following us home! It was so ridiculous that I wasn't sure I wanted to return the next week. Still, my strong skepticism had been shaken by what had happened—and most of all I wanted to find out how it was done.

On the way home, Dorothy and I discussed the evening. "They must have some very elaborate equipment," I said, "in order to produce all those alleged phenomena. It must be in the attic right over the room or in the basement under it. Next week I'll ask if I can look around."

Dorothy shook her head. "What possible reason would they have to fake a seance like that? There was no admission charge or love offering, and they certainly didn't try to convert us to spiritualism."

"It's very strange," I replied. "Wait a minute, though! I'll bet tonight was a preliminary for the setup. Next week they'll ask us for a donation and we'll also be asked to join the spiritualist church."

"Didn't they seem like honest and sincere people to you?"

"Well, yes," I countered, "but any intelligent person can't accept. . . ."

She interrupted me. "Next week you'll have to find someone else to go with you. It makes me very nervous to have my beads flicked up and down, and that yellow light next to you was eerie. Furthermore, if we do have any visitors not from this world tonight, you'll have to take me to the funny farm."

I laughed. "Nonsense! But maybe your mom and your Aunt Lou would like to come with me next week. Perhaps your dad and Uncle Frank will whisper over the trumpets." Both Dorothy's father and her Uncle Frank had died several years previously.

2

"Don't Turn Off the Light"

After a long drive home we collapsed into bed, exhausted, but were too stimulated to sleep. So again we discussed the evening's adventure.

Suddenly there were three sharp raps on the ceiling. "Turn on the light," Dorothy quavered.

This I did promptly, muttering "Pitch pockets. The house is still new, only about three years old. The wood is drying out. That's the noise we hear."

Again, three sharp raps! But this time they were on the nightstand next to my side of the bed and they produced chills up my spine. I knew well enough they were not from pitch pockets.

"Gotta get a drink of water," I heard my dry voice say, and I started to get out of bed.

Dorothy's hand gripped my arm like a vise. "You're going nowhere," she said. "You'll stay here with me and listen to the pitch pockets."

By this time rappings were coming from the walls, the ceiling, the floor, and the bedroom furniture. They went on for about ten minutes before stopping.

"It's probably someone playing tricks on us," I said bravely. "I'll just get the flashlight and look around outside the house. You can come with me if you like."

"No thanks," was her reply. "Who would be playing tricks at three o'clock in the morning? Furthermore, those raps were on the inside of the room."

"It did sound that way. Anyhow, they've stopped now, so let's get some sleep." I reached over to turn out the lamp.

"Don't turn off the light," she ordered, so I left it burning.

Eventually, I dropped off to sleep, awakening a few hours later unrefreshed and vividly remembering a dream I had been dreaming in which Mr. Reiner had been shaped like a seance trumpet, darting from wall to ceiling to floor to furniture, striking his head to produce loud raps and knocks.

The next day I eagerly told our friends, and anyone else who would listen to me, what amazing things had happened to us the previous night. Some looked at me with pity, some with amusement, and a few with interest. I mentally noted those who listened with interest. They might be candidates for future trips with me to the seance room.

A few days later, in a restaurant, I ran into one of our city's leading psychiatrists. Of course, I told him about our adventures at the seance.

He laughed and said, "Richard, you have been the victim of a fraud. Let me explain what happened to you."

He took out his pen and on a napkin he sketched the main trunk of the central nervous system. "Note the sheath on the nerve," he said. "The room is dark and warm and the medium's voice is droning on and on. The sheath is wearing thin and you have become hypnotized. The medium is suggesting that you are hearing the noises and feeling your body being touched. In truth, none of these things are really happening."

This sounded logical and scientific, but had I really been hypnotized? I certainly had not. There was something wrong with his explanation even though I had no better answer.

"What if I take a tape recorder with me next week and tape the entire session?" I asked.

"It's very doubtful if they will allow you to do this. They know there would be nothing on the tape when you play it back, except your own voices and that of the medium making suggestions."

"You're probably right," I agreed, "but just the same I'll ask him if I can tape. If he lets me, I'll give you a report."

The psychiatrist laughed. "Don't bother. There's only one explanation and I have already given it to you."

3

The Apport

Apport: The dematerialization of objects such as stones, flowers, coins, birds, animals, etc., and the transportation and rematerialization of these items through solid wall by supernormal means.

Dorothy's mother, Frances, and her Aunt Lou decided to accompany me on my forthcoming trip to the seance. They seemed excited but also a bit apprehensive. I had called Mr. Reiner and asked if I could bring the two ladies instead of Dorothy. He agreed and then asked if we had had visitors after arriving home.

"We certainly had something, Mr. Reiner." I then related what had occurred.

"Something like that usually happens," he said. "I hope it didn't disturb Mrs. Walker too much. Actually, the rappings were made by personalities who had been close to you on the earth plane. They were trying to attract your attention and desperately wanted you to know that they are not dead, but just living in a different state of consciousness than we do."

Though this was a happy explanation, I could not accept it. I then asked Mr. Reiner if I could tape the session at the next sitting. "You certainly may," he replied. "Many of our guests bring tape recorders. We have no objections."

Thanking him politely, I said we were looking forward to enjoying the fellowship at the meeting next Tuesday evening.

On the appointed evening, the two ladies and I were warmly greeted by the Reiners and Mrs. Reiner's sister, who was visiting from out-of-state. Only the six of us would be sitting tonight, they said.

When Frances saw the oil paintings on the walls of the seance room, she became pale and gasped, "Why, the eyes in those pictures are *alive!*"

"They certainly are," echoed her sister Lou. It was obvious that Lou was not so disturbed as Frances.

As at our first visit, Mr. Reiner explained the significance of the paintings and the reason for the toy instruments and paper pads on the floor. They asked me to sit between them and requested to hold my hand if the going "got rough." I placed the tape recorder under my chair and turned it to *Record.* Since it had an hour's tape, I could get a good portion of the session.

Mr. Reiner snapped off the light as before, and we recited the Lord's Prayer. Then for the next ten minutes we chatted in the dark until, "Welcome, Dr. Chin," said our host.

"I see a light shaped like a person!" exclaimed my mother-in-law.

"I see a light too," said Aunt Lou.

I strained my eyes but saw absolutely nothing except the luminous bands on the trumpets which were streaking through the air. Immediately the toy instruments started playing, and again somebody or something placed the xylophone on my lap. The noise was even worse than the preceding week. A trumpet was tapping my knee at the same time somebody or something was stroking my head.

Suddenly Frances let out a piercing scream. "No, no!" she cried. "Please don't touch me! I can't stand it! Turn on the lights!" She started to sob.

"Nothing is going to hurt you," said Mr. Reiner, "but I'll turn on the lights if you wish."

The two trumpets dropped to the floor with a noisy clatter and the light went on. The toy instruments were all over the floor as before. So were the paper pads and pencils. The xylophone was still on my lap but the mallet was lying at my feet.

It was apparent that whoever had been playing the instruments had made a very hurried departure. Where had they gone? Anyone walking on that floor in the dark would have stepped on the musical toys and crushed them. However, this we would have heard because there was no carpeting on the floor. I decided that when the sitting was over, I would ask Mr. Reiner if I could check his basement and attic. It was time to get to the bottom of this mystery.

Mr. Reiner led Frances into the living room, seated her in a comfortable chair, gave her a magazine to read, and returned to the seance room.

Frances later told us that she wished she had never left the seance room. The moment she was left alone in the living room, a rocking chair near her started to rock and it went on rocking. Then there were loud rappings on the table by her chair. All this continued until the sitting was over and we came into the living room where she was. She wanted to cry for help but was too embarrassed to do this as she had already interrupted the sitting once. So she sat there, all alone, in terror and perspiration, and prayed.

Meanwhile, in the seance room, things were also happening. As soon as Reiner turned out the light once more, we were all being patted and stroked again and the toy instruments were being violently played. I felt the cold aluminum of the trumpet slide gently up and down my cheek. Again I started experimenting as I had at the first sitting. I gave mental commands: Stop! Start! Stop! Start! It was astounding; all the commands were immediately obeyed.

Suddenly Aunt Lou exclaimed, "My goodness, someone put a flower in my hand! I think it's—uh—yes, it smells like a rose!"

Mrs. Reiner was delighted. "You have an apport! This is a gift from your husband. He has been lovingly stroking your hair. How wonderful! Apports are very rare. This is the first time a flower has come through. On rare occasions our sitters have been given feathers from their Indian spirit guide. . . Oh, I'm so happy for you!"

The bedlam of music abruptly ceased and whispering began to come from the trumpet. We strained our ears but couldn't make it out.

"Can you understand it?" I asked Reiner.

"All I can get is, 'It's Frank, Frank!' "

"Frank was my husband's name," said Lou with emotion. (I should point out that we had been careful not to reveal the names of the deceased husbands.) More mind reading, I thought, but how was it done?

Another half hour of noise, caresses and unintelligible whispers from the trumpets, and then Mr. Reiner said, "They are leaving now."

One by one the instruments fell to the floor and were silent; the trumpets were pulled apart and clattered to the floor.

"Goodby, Dr. Chin," said Reiner.

"Goodby, Dr. Chin," we repeated. We recited the Twenty-Third Psalm in unison before our host turned on the light. No messages tonight and no names of spirit guides had been written on the pads of paper which were strewn all over the floor.

But there sat Aunt Lou holding a beautiful red rose. Tears in her eyes, she said, "Thank you, Frank."*

I picked up my recorder and we went into the living room to join Frances. She was sitting very erect, her hands clutching the arms of the chair. Her eyes showed fright. Her face was wet with perspiration.

"I didn't think you would ever get here!" she gasped. "Look at the rocking chair!" It was gently rocking. While we watched, it slowed, then stopped.

"And all that rapping!" cried Frances, "I'm a nervous wreck!"

"I'm truly sorry, Mrs. Zeller," said Mrs. Reiner. "We shouldn't have left you out here alone. Please believe me, the spirits meant no harm. They were trying to tell you they love you."

When Mrs. Reiner left the room to prepare the refreshments, I asked Mr. Reiner if I could look in the basement and in the attic. He rather sadly said, "Yes, but I'm afraid you'll get your clothes dirty. There's no basement, only a crawlspace, and the attic is unfinished."

"That doesn't matter. I'll run out to the car and get my flashlight."

"No need to, I'll get you the one out of our bedroom." As he left, the thought flashed through my mind that he would also take this opportunity to disconnect the wiring to the apparatus that produced the phenomena.

He returned, handed me his flashlight, and took me to the stairs leading up to the attic. He offered to come with me but I said no, thinking he would be embarrassed when I made my discovery. So, up the stairs I went. I flashed the light to the area which I judged was approximately over the seance room.

---

*When Aunt Lou arrived home she placed the rose next to her husband's picture which is on the fireplace mantel. Today, some twenty years later, the rose is still there, faded and dry, but strangely unwilted!

All I saw was floor joists and a plank to walk on. Sheetrock was visible between the joists. Nothing else but cobwebs—several of which I inhaled.

Hm, I mused. Then it's under the house. This is only a strike. I'm not struck out, yet.

My host was waiting for me at the bottom of the stairs. Brushing the cobwebs from my clothes, he remarked, "I'm glad you didn't fall through the sheetrock. Some of those planks are a little wobbly up there. . .All right, now, the crawlspace under the house. We'll have to go outside to get to it."

Fortunately it wasn't raining. He took me to a small door under the house, barely large enough to allow my corpulent body to enter.

"I hate to see you go in there," he said. "You'll get filthy and I don't expect you'll find anything, although we did hear some noise under the house a few nights ago." Aha, I thought, he doesn't want me to see what he has under there.

"That's all right, Mr. Reiner," I said. "I have to settle an argument with a friend at home, so if you don't mind, I'll go in." I was lying. There was no argument. It was an agreement that I was to bring back proof.

The crawlspace was much worse than the attic. I had to crawl halfway under the house to get under the seance room, and down there the spider webs were much thicker and much stickier. I had to make my way around several concrete piers. Furthermore, I had a strong feeling I had company in there—and it wasn't Mr. Reiner.

Finally I arrived at the area I felt needed examining. Again I found nothing. There were no holes in the subflooring, no trap door, no wires. I was now in a dilemma. I couldn't quite accept the explanation of my psychiatrist friend—although I thought I would know after playing back the tape. At the same time I couldn't quite accept Mr. Reiner's spiritualistic interpretation either. At the moment, however, I was becoming claustrophobic. I felt an urgent need to remove myself from this location.

Then I heard a noise. It was close—a sort of growling hiss. I shined the light in the direction of the sound and my heart stopped.

There in the light-beam I saw two eyes, and below the eyes an obscene mouth full of sharp teeth. I yelled, "Get out of the way, Mr. Reiner! I'm coming out!"

Then I saw the body behind the head. It was a possum— and a granddaddy! I was partially relieved and my retreat was not quite as fast as I had planned it. Still I cracked my head and skinned the knuckles on both hands. I didn't know possums hissed. Perhaps they don't, yet this one did.

When I told Mr. Reiner about his crawlspace tenant, he said, "So that was the noise we heard the other night. I'll set a trap for him tomorrow." At the end of the evening I told him I would very likely come alone next week, but the following Tuesday, with his permission, I would like to bring a couple of friends with me.

"Your friends are always welcome...and by the way, Dick, why don't you call me by my first name, Mark?"

"Thanks so much, Mark, and I'll bring the ice cream."

By now I genuinely liked the Reiners. They were warm, personable, intelligent people. Still, I couldn't agree with their spiritualistic philosophy, though I was beginning to feel that they were not involved in any chicanery.

My clothes were a mess. On the way home, the ladies remarked that besides not looking tidy, I had somehow developed a peculiarly unpleasant odor. I had to agree with them. "In my visit to the possum's habitat tonight," I said, "I apparently crawled through something to remember him by."

I took the ladies home and found Dorothy waiting up for me when I arrived at our house. I triumphantly waved the tape recorder at her. "Now we'll find out if I was hypnotized or hallucinating." I pushed the *Play* button.

For an hour we listened to the sounds from the seance room. It was all on tape just as we had heard it the first time—the musical bedlam, the trumpets clattering, the whispering voices we couldn't understand.

It was clear that my doctor friend had been wrong about that. Nevertheless, I felt that further research was definitely in order.

Auntie Has a Visitor

The next morning, Aunt Lou telephoned and announced that she had had a sleepless night. She was an omnivorous reader. She would always read in bed for an hour or so before going to sleep; last night, though, she had no sooner picked up her book than the bed started to shake violently.

Earthquake, she thought. But, no, the rest of the room was not vibrating, only the bed. Then it had to be a visitor. Mr. Reiner had said she might expect this.

She felt some uneasiness, just the same. Her uneasiness turned to alarm when she saw a sudden indentation in the bedcovers at the bottom of the bed, as if someone invisible had sat down on it. To make matters even worse, the bed itself was now shaking so turbulently that she was becoming nauseated.

"Please stop!" she cried. The bed seemed to shake even more.

In desperation she called out, "In the name of Jesus Christ, leave me alone!" Abruptly, the bed stopped shaking. With a prayerful sigh of relief, Aunt Lou picked up her book again and attempted to read.

But she could not read. She remembered again that Mr. Reiner had said her husband would try very hard to let her know that he was with her, and that something might happen after she arrived home.

This thought, however, was no comfort. When the bed had been shaking so terribly, she hadn't felt Frank's presence in the room at all. Whatever—or whoever—had been causing the bed to shake, and the indentation to appear at the foot of it, had certainly not seemed to have her interest at heart.

Why would she have been so terrified if it had been Frank trying to attract her attention? Also, what about those loud knocks and raps which the Walkers had heard in their bedroom last week? So far, she had to admit, it seemed that Mr. Reiner was accurately calling his shots—but was his explanation of all these phenomena correct?

Aunt Lou rather doubted it.

4

Do Not Test Us

When Tuesday arrived I made the trip alone as predicted. The school principal and his wife were back, making a total of five people for the sitting.

Dr. Chin was in. . .and as usual the toy xylophone was on my lap, and being played violently. I reached out quickly and my fingers closed over a hand. It was large and warm and was holding the mallet that was striking the keys.

Just as I had thought! It was a fake after all and I had caught someone.

My hand began to feel its way along the hand I was grasping. Suddenly, I realized there was no wrist, no arm! There was nothing but the hand! At that moment the hand pulled away from mine with such force that, had I hung on, I'm sure my arm could have been pulled from its socket.

I sat there bewildered, my skepticism more than a little bruised. Then I heard a pencil writing on paper in the air near my right ear. After a couple of moments I felt a piece of paper touch my hand, which was still aching from the wrench it had received.

I took the paper, but had to hold it until the lights were back on. Sure enough, there was a message for me. It was beautifully printed in a style which I did not recognize.

It said: *Do not test us. We will test you.*

It was signed, Kado Dos.

I had now encountered an unfriendly hand, with abnormal strength, suspended in the air—and received a reprimand from Mr. Dos, my alleged spirit guide! Were more bizarre adventures forthcoming? Little did I know then that they were just starting!

I was feeling a little guilty because we had been told not to experiment when a medium was producing phenomena. It was possible for the medium to be severely injured, or even killed, if a light should be turned on when the medium was in a condition of trance, or when psychic fluid* had left his body. At that time I doubted this, but subsequently I have found that it is true.

---

*Psychic fluid is a mysterious substance sometimes called ectoplasm. It is defined in Norman Blunsdon's *A Dictionary of Modern Spiritualism:* "A subtle living matter present in the physical body primarily invisible but capable of assuming vaporous, liquid, or solid states and properties. It is extruded usually in the dark from the pores and various orifices of the body, and is slightly luminous, the more so when condensed.

"The temperature of the room is usually lowered when ectoplasm is produced; it possesses a characteristic smell and is cold to the touch. This substance is held to be responsible for the production of all phenomena classed as 'physical!' " According to Blunsdon, ectoplasm flowing from the medium's body forms into elastic or rigid rods to produce movement in objects, all types of noises and artificial "voice boxes!" This material, which may also take the shape of faces, limbs and occasionally whole bodies, is produced by the subconscious mind of the medium.

5

Cold Ankles and the Birthday Cake

My adventures in this new land I was exploring had aroused the curiosity of two old friends of mine. These were men eminently successful in their business careers. Ron owned a huge electronics factory and Bill was a real estate broker. Both had more than a normal share of curiosity (also a problem of mine) and their inquisitiveness had been channeled into energies which had produced fortunes for both.

It was these two men whom I now wanted to take with me to a sitting.

When I called Mr. Reiner to double check, he again graciously said he would be happy for me to bring friends. In attendance, he said, would also be a young man who was a psychology major in a nearby college. Because the next Tuesday, the day of the sitting, would be this young man's twenty-first birthday, Reiner said that a birthday celebration would be in order. If my friends Ron and Bill had known the nature of the celebration that was to take place, I believe they would have stayed at home that Tuesday evening!

When we went into the seance room, there was a large birthday cake on a glass platter in the middle of the floor, in addition to the usual paraphernalia which we always found there. Seven plates were stacked beside the cake. Seven forks lay on the top plate. There was also a huge, wicked-looking butcher knife that must have been at least twenty-four inches long. Mrs. Reiner's sister, Laurel, was sitting with us tonight, making a total of seven in attendance.

Before we went into the seance room, however, we had a short chat with Leonard, the college student. We discovered that he had been sitting for three years. A psychology major and also a spiritualist? How ridiculous!

Leonard also told us that his uncle had been an assistant to the famous Dr. Rine at Duke University and it was through this uncle that he had become interested in parapsychology and related subjects. Leonard felt that only at the Reiners' was there a complete absence of fraud in these matters.

"No," he smiled, in reply to Ron's inquiry, "I'm not a spiritualist although I find I am leaning slightly that way. The things that happen here are in complete conflict with my major at school. I'm hoping that someday there will be a semblance of compatibility between these two diametrically opposite areas."

In the seance room, my friends Ron and Bill were seated across the circle from me. As usual, I sat next to Mr. Reiner, whose heavy breathing I could always hear. (I suspected that he had some type of asthmatic condition.) At that time I was still slightly suspicious that upon occasion he might leave his chair and somehow produce the phenomena we were observing. A few times, when I had not heard his breathing, I "accidentally" moved my arm or leg in his direction. Each· time I did this, I came into contact with some part of Mr. Reiner.

Still, even though I was growing more and more convinced that the Reiners would not stoop to any kind of chicanery, my reason would ask, "How can any of these things occur?"

On this Tuesday evening, we had all been sitting in the dark for nearly half an hour and I was getting impatient for our so-called spirit friends to make an appearance. Suddenly I felt a cold breeze on my ankles. At the same time, Ron, Bill and I asked in unison, "Where does this cold breeze come from?"

Leonard spoke up. "We don't really know but very often just before materialization occurs, you will feel a cold breeze on your ankles."

No sooner had Leonard made this statement than Mr. Reiner said, "Welcome, Dr. Chin." The trumpets darted from one side of the room to the other, and the toy instruments began to make their loud, discordant noise.

Suddenly Ron exclaimed nervously, "Hey, somebody's patting my head!"

Mr. Reiner said, "Ron, there's a man standing by your chair. He's very tall and thin and has curly white hair over his ears. The rest of his head is bald. He's wearing white overalls and has a large red pencil in his breast pocket."

Ron, his voice trembling, exclaimed, "Why, that's Dad Willard, my wife's father! Dad Willard died only three months ago!"

Mrs. Reiner, her sister, and Leonard all remarked that they could see a white light by the chair upon which Ron was sitting. I strained my eyes but could see nothing except the two luminous bands around the trumpets, which were now stationary in the middle of the room, about four feet above the floor.

Suddenly I felt pressure on my knees. It was the birthday cake, which had been placed on my lap! I could feel the glass plate and I could smell the fragrant chocolate frosting. I announced that I had the cake in my possession. Instantly it was jerked off my lap. Ron said it was now in his lap. It could not have taken more than half a second for the cake to travel from my lap to Ron's.

Then I felt something pushed into my hand—the handle of the wicked-looking butcher knife which had been lying on the floor next to the cake.

"Wait a minute!" I exclaimed. "I have the knife in my hand now."

"Which end?" asked Ron.

"It's the handle, thank God."

Instantly the knife was dragged out of my hand with unbelievable force. If someone had pulled it away from me, I thought, he had hold of the cutting end and must have been severely cut—but nobody cried out. (I made a mental note to take a quick look for blood on the floor when the sitting was over.)

With absolutely no time lapse, Bill said in a quivering voice, "Now I have the knife, and I don't like this at all. A big, sharp knife flying through the air in the dark. Someone could be badly hurt! It also makes me very nervous to be patted and stroked like this. Frankly, I'm not enjoying this experience."

Mrs. Reiner replied, "Please don't be alarmed, Bill. Whoever is touching you is trying to demonstrate his love for you. At one time he was probably very close to you on earth. However, if it disturbs you, just ask that the patting be stopped—either audibly or mentally—and it will. Please don't be worried about the knife either. No one has ever been injured in a seance, except the medium."*

---

*Scientific researchers of psychic phenomena have weighed sensitives in their normal state, and also when they have been producing phenomena. It appears that a vaporous fluid leaves the body through the orifices and forms into levers, hands, faces, and other parts of the human body. When this

The cake and the knife went all the way around the room. One after another, each was in possession of both very briefly. There had been whisperings from both trumpets, but no one could understand the words, including Mr. Reiner himself, except once. According to Reiner, one of the trumpets whispered, "Happy Birthday, Leonard."

Bill and Ron, the newcomers, had been given slips of paper upon which they could read the names of their spirit guides when the lights were turned on again. The noise from the toy instruments was diminishing and the trumpets had been pulled apart and had clattered to the floor. I felt a plate being pushed into my hand and heard the sound of a fork being placed on the plate.

"They are leaving now," said Mr. Reiner. "Goodnight, Dr. Chin. Now let us recite the Twenty-Third Psalm together."

Then the lights went on. Each one was holding a plate, upon which was a piece of cake and a fork. The cake had been perfectly cut; all pieces appeared to be exactly the same size.

The remaining half of the cake was on the glass platter in the middle of the floor, just where we had seen it at the beginning of the sitting. The long, sharp butcher knife had been carefully placed on the glass platter, beside the cake.

I picked up the knife and examined it closely. There was not a crumb on the blade, nor any sign of the frosting from

fluid, which is known as psychic fluid or ectoplasm, leaves the medium's body, a weight loss of from seven to ten pounds occurs. At this time, the sensitive appears to be vulnerable and in danger of harm, especially if a light is suddenly flashed on.

At a recent seance in New York, it is reported that a guest sitter flicked his cigarette lighter on, close to the medium's face. The medium suffered a coronary occlusion from which he did not recover. There are many similar cases on record. Not all were fatal, but in all cases severe injury resulted. Most mediums produce materialization phenomena only in the dark, leaving them open to suspicion of fraud. However, a few can produce phenomena when the room is lighted with a red light. Only rarely can phenomena be produced in a normally lighted room.

the cake. I could see no indication whatever that the butcher knife had been used to cut the cake. Nor was there any residue on the cake platter. There was not a single crumb— only the remaining half of the cake.

On the way home, Bill said that this was his first seance— and his last one. Ron said he would like to return but not with his wife. If she had been there tonight when her father came through, she would have become hyper-emotionalized.

6

The Psychiatrist's Dilemma

Earlier, I wrote about my psychiatrist friend, Dr. Jack, who patiently explained to me how all seances were fraudulent and that, if a session were tape-recorded, only *our* voices would be on the tape. The whispering voices from the trumpets, the noise from the toy musical instruments, the sounds of the trumpets being pulled apart, and their sections falling to the floor—all these sounds would not be on the tape, because we were hallucinating.

Perhaps even mass hallucination was occurring, he said, if all the people who were present thought they were hearing the same things. He assured me authoritatively that the hallucination would have been brought on by suggestion from the medium.

You will recall, though, that I did tape a sitting and that everything was on the tape just as we heard it in the seance room. So, armed with this knowledge, I called my friend at his home one evening several weeks later and told him that I had seance material on a tape, which would be of great interest to him.

The Psychiatrist's Dilemma

35

He sighed. "Richard, you are a die-hard. All right, bring your recorder over tonight and we'll listen to it, if you insist. I'll explain it all to you again, and perhaps this time I can convince you that all so-called psychic phenomena are fraudulent."

So I took the tape recorder over and we sat down together and played the tape. I noted with satisfaction that he was listening attentively and, I thought, with considerable interest. We finished the tape. Switching off the recorder, I turned to him.

He said, "All right, so you weren't hallucinating. Obviously your medium and his wife—who is his accomplice—are whispering through the trumpets and they are playing the musical instruments. They are also waving the trumpets in the air."

"Impossible," I said. "When all this is going on, I'm talking to them. When they answer me, I can tell they are still in their chairs."

"You just think they're in their chairs," he countered. "They have given you the suggestion that they are in their chairs. They have hypnotized you into thinking they are in their chairs. But wait a minute! There is another possibility. They both may have telescopic metal rods, similar to automobile antennas. If they have, these are hidden in their clothes. Then when the light is turned off, they attach these rods to the trumpets, or to the luminous bands that are around the trumpets, and wave them in the air. These same rods are attached to the toy musical instruments."

"Maybe," I replied, "but I don't think so. Listen here, what do you charge your patients per hour?"

"Fifty dollars," he said.

"All right, I'll make you a proposition. Let me pick you up after dinner next Tuesday. We'll go to the seance together. Let's see—it will take about an hour and a quarter to get there. The sitting lasts about an hour and a half, then a half hour for refreshments and an hour and a quarter to get home. That's a total of four and a half hours. Now then, listen. If you feel it's really a fake, I'll pay you the $225 for your time."

He looked skeptical. "And will you also pay for both of our admission fees?"

"There's no admission fee."

"No fee?" For the first time a small feather crack appeared in his cement-like confidence. "All right. It's a deal," he said. "Pick me up at six-thirty next Tuesday evening."

I could see in his eyes that he was already depositing my $225 check in his personal bank account, and I wondered if I had made a grievous error. That amount of money would make a terrible dent in our savings account.

I called Mr. Reiner and asked it I could bring my highly skeptical psychiatrist friend to the sitting next Tuesday. He said, "He will be welcome. Most of our guests who attend their first sittings are very skeptical. And some of them remain that way. However, I will appreciate it if your friend will refrain from any active experimenting during the sitting. If a light is suddenly flashed on, you know, this could result in great physical harm to me."

The doctor was waiting on his front porch as I drove up to his house on Tuesday evening. He was holding a brown paper bag, and the sight of it made me feel a little uneasy. As he was getting into the car I asked, "What's in the sack, Jack? Your lunch?"

He gave me a sour look. "In this sack," he said deliberately, "I have a pair of infrared glasses which will enable me to see in the dark. I will give you a running commentary on the alleged phenomena and will explain to you the tricks the medium is using."

He looked at me coldly. "I presume you brought your checkbook with you. You'll be needing it when we get home tonight."

Ouch! This was an unexpected turn, and it might prove very embarrassing. Still, I had promised Mr. Reiner that the doctor would not experiment during the sitting. "I'm sorry, Jack," I said flatly, "but you'll have to leave the glasses in the car."

"Absolutely not," he said, and started to get out of the car.

"Wait a minute. Let's discuss this reasonably." I was frantically trying to think of a way to save the situation.

"There is nothing to discuss, Walker," he said. "Either I'm going to wear these glasses at your meeting or I'm staying home."

"Why don't you hide them under your coat, then, and when the lights are turned off you can put them on, and no one will be the wiser."

"No, sir, I will not resort to subterfuge," he said. I had to admire his openness, even though I was obviously losing this round. I had to make one last try.

"When we get to the Reiners' home, may I ask him if you can wear the glasses?" I asked. "Then if he says no, will you please leave them in the car?"

"If he says no," Dr. Jack replied, "I will leave the glasses in the car and you will pay me $225 for my time." I agreed. I had no choice. Neither of us was in a happy mood, so the drive down was sober and silent.

After introducing Dr. Jack to Mr. Reiner, I asked with considerable trepidation, if Dr. Jack could wear the infrared glasses. I was much relieved—and somewhat surprised—when Reiner turned to the doctor and said,

"Yes, indeed, you may wear the glasses, sir. It may interest you to know that in the not too distant future we will be allowed to have a red light on when we are holding a sitting."

A flicker of surprise crossed the stiffly skeptical countenance of Dr. Jack, and I couldn't help emitting a sigh of relief. Things seemed to be going a little better now. Of course, the evening was far from over.

The psychiatrist thoroughly examined the seance room. He knocked on the floors and the walls. He checked the locations of the studs in the walls, for some unknown reason. He stood on the chair and ran his fingers over the ceiling, then glanced at the spirit paintings and muttered, "Poor work but the eyes are interesting."

At last he sat down in a chair across the room from me. He put on the infrared goggles and said, "I'm ready. You can start your funny business."

I felt that Dr. Jack's behavior was demeaning and rude, but the Reiners didn't appear to notice and were their usual charming and hospitable selves. Reiner turned off the lights, and everyone except Dr. Jack chatted for a few moments before Reiner announced the appearance of Dr. Chin. The trumpets left the floor and as usual darted rapidly around the room, following the same pattern as at the previous sittings. The toy musical instruments went into their discordant racket.

Suddenly in a tone near to hysteria, Dr. Jack yelled, "Stop this immediately! I want the lights on now!"

"Just a moment, Doctor," said Mr. Reiner.

But Dr. Jack didn't want to wait the moment. He leaped from his chair and started in the general direction of the light switch, which was on the wall next to the door near Reiner's chair. He tripped and fell down with a tremendous thud that jarred the entire room.

Immediately, Mr. Reiner turned on the lights, and it was difficult not to laugh at the sight that met our eyes. Dr. Jack lay spread-eagled on the floor, face down. One of the trumpets was rakishly perched on his head, giving the exact impression of a dunce cap. The infrared goggles had slipped down under his nose, and somehow two toy drums had landed on his backside.

After Mr. Reiner and I helped him to his feet, he shrugged off our anxious questions and grimly started to examine the trumpets and other items which were lying on the floor. He then turned to our host and said, "With these glasses I could see everything going on in this room, and I want to know what you have done with the levers and hands that I saw manipulating the trumpets and toys. I saw a human head, too, with no body, suspended in the air next to Mrs. Reiner."

"If you will pardon my repeating, Doctor," said Mr. Reiner, "we are not involved in chicanery of any kind here. The phenomena you observe are genuine. You may evaluate them as you see fit. Now, if you wish to continue your sitting with us, will you please remain in your chair? Or perhaps you'd rather go into the living room."

I secretly wished that Jack would go into the living room. Perhaps the chair would rock, as it had for my mother-in-law, and the loud rappings would be heard on the furniture. I was intensely curious to know how he would interpret these phenomena.

But, no, Jack elected to stay with us. He sat down in his chair, adjusted his goggles, and commanded, "You may turn off the lights now." A fraction of a second after the lights were off, the noises started again and the trumpets flew around the room.

Dr. Jack seemed to be talking to himself. I heard him say, "Remarkable! Look at that small hand—it must be a child's holding that mouth organ. But who is blowing it? Oh, now I see. There's a mouth. It's part of a face. Incredible! Oh, oh, here comes the trumpet. It's patting my head—not so hard, please! That's better. It looks like a lever made out of human flesh that's attached to this trumpet. What? What did you say?"

There was whispering from the trumpet and we all clearly heard, "Jung was right."

Dr. Jack was indignant. "Jung was wrong. Even Freud was closer to the truth than Jung."

From the trumpet again, the whisper, "Jung was right. Jung was right. Jung was right." Apparently, the whisperer had faith in the great Swiss psychologist.

The trumpet left Jack and tapped my knee. "Any message for me tonight?" I asked. No response. The trumpets flew to the ceiling, and we could see the two luminous bands now stationary there. Both trumpets apparently stayed together immobile in the air near the ceiling.

The toy xylophone was now on my lap. Dr. Jack, in a dull voice, said, "There is a hand holding each mallet and I note with interest that's all—just hands."

Mrs. Reiner said, " I see a white light near the door by my husband."

"No," said Dr. Jack, "it's not a light. I see an elderly Oriental man in a white robe standing there. Let me take off these glasses and maybe I'll see a light.—No, I don't see anything. I'll put them on again. . . . That's funny, he's gone."

"He's still here," said Mr. Reiner, "but they're all going to leave now."

"Astounding!" gasped Dr. Jack. "I see hands and strange objects and parts of bodies in the air! All moving rapidly toward Mr. Reiner!—Now they're gone."

"Goodnight, Dr. Chin," said Mr. Reiner. "Now will you all please recite with me the Twenty-Third Psalm?"

Dr. Jack seemed reluctant to leave the seance room after the lights were turned on again. He spent several minutes staring intently at the spirit paintings on the walls. He again carefully examined each toy musical instrument and both trumpets that had been pulled apart and had clattered to the floor just before Reiner said goodnight to Dr. Chin.

Mrs. Reiner announced that refreshments were ready. Dr. Jack said he was not hungry and asked if he could stay in the seance room and ponder while we went to the living room for a short chew-and-chat session. While we were eating, we heard the Doctor apparently talking to himself in the seance room.

"I'm a little worried about your friend, Dr. Jack," Mr. Reiner said to me. "We've had several scientists and medical men sit with us, but Dr. Jack is the first psychiatrist we've ever had attend one of our sessions. I hope this experience won't require him to seek help from one of his professional associates."

On the way home, my attempts to engage Jack in conversation were futile. He made one remark—the last words I ever heard him utter. He said, with considerable bitterness, "I went to school for ten years in preparation for my profession. And now, in this one miserable evening, thanks to you, Walker, that whole decade of education has been blown. I would prefer never to talk to you again."

When we arrived at his house, he opened the car door and without a word got out and slammed it so hard I was afraid the window would break. I was saddened by his attitude, but I couldn't suppress a small feeling of triumph at the success of the evening's seance. And he hadn't asked for my check of $225!

Fourteen years went by with no word from Dr. Jack. Then a few months ago, I read his obituary in the newspaper. I couldn't help wondering if he knows now whether Jung was right or wrong.

7

A Strange Bedfellow for Elizabeth

Among our friends is a delightful lady of great beauty and high intelligence. She was a Phi Beta Kappa at Reed College, and earned a Master's degree in English Literature. Reared a Roman Catholic, she is deeply religious; but still is unable to accept the traditional dogma of the Church. She was eager to explore the new frontier of psychic research.

When I told Elizabeth about my seance experience, she exclaimed with great enthusiasm, "I'm ready! Can we go tonight?"

"Sorry," I replied. "I'll be tied up every night for two weeks. If you wish, I'll telephone Mr. Reiner and ask if you and Conrad can attend next Tuesday night's sitting." Conrad, her husband, is not interested in psychic matters. He actually disbelieves anything pertaining to the occult.

"No, I don't believe Conrad would be willing to go, but I'd like to have my dear friend and neighbor, Marilyn, go with me, if that would be all right with Mr. Reiner. Please make the call and say we'll be there, ready for anything!"

I set up the appointment for the two ladies as requested; then didn't hear from Elizabeth again until early the following

Wednesday morning. In fact, our phone rang at seven o'clock. Elizabeth's soft, well-modulated voice said, "Richard, I have had the most extraordinary experience. It culminated with Wallace as my bed partner and, my, how he snores!"

My ears must be deceiving me, I thought. The Elizabeth I knew was a lady of the highest moral standards, and under no circumstances would she ever, ever, compromise her principles.

"I'm not with you, Elizabeth. Who is Wallace and what's this bed-partner business?" I knew that Elizabeth and Conrad, for most of their thirty years of married life, had preferred to sleep apart, in separate bedrooms. But someone named Wallace had been snoring last night in Elizabeth's bed?

Elizabeth laughed. "Calm down, Richard," she said. "I will explain. The seance was simply sensational. We were patted, caressed, whispered to. Music—if you can call it that—was played to us. Mrs. Reiner makes delicious chocolate cake, and my spirit guide's name is Wallace. Yes, sir, and Wallace slept in my bed last night and he snores worse than Conrad. Your friends, the Reiners, are lovely, sincere people. Mr. Reiner has a remarkable talent. Marilyn and I feel he is scrupulously honest, even though we don't, as yet, feel we can accept his interpretation for the remarkable things that occurred."

Elizabeth then described in detail all the events that had taken place at the sitting. They were similar to those I had experienced.

"Now, Richard," Elizabeth went on, "I think we have a problem. I had no sooner turned out my bed lamp than tremendous snoring assailed my ears. The noise was right next to me in my bed. "I turned over and said, 'I didn't hear you come in, Conrad. Goodness, wake up and take your snores back to your own bedroom.' Then I gave him a poke with my elbow.

"But he wasn't there! I turned on the light and, by golly, Richard, there was no one there! I pulled the covers back and there was an indentation as if someone invisible were lying there. I put my hand on the indentation and felt nothing. But the sheet was warm! And the snoring continued!

"Then all of a sudden the snoring stopped," went on Elizabeth, not giving me time to comment. "A deep, male voice said, 'Don't be afraid, it's only me. Wallace.' The snoring immediately started again. Okay, Wallace, I thought. If you want to stick around I guess it's all right. But you're not going to disturb my sleep. And I pulled the covers over me and turned out the light.

"Frankly, I didn't get to sleep for a couple of hours because of the snoring. This really was a rather unearthly experience! When I woke up this morning, the snoring had stopped and there was no indentation on my bed."

"Elizabeth," I said, "do you think you could have been dreaming all this?"

"Absolutely not," she said firmly. "I must now prepare Conrad's breakfast and I will tell him about snoring Wallace. If he comes again tonight, I will call you tomorrow morning and give you a report."

I didn't expect a call but it came.

"All right, Richard," Elizabeth started in, "first of all, my husband thinks we're both nuts. But then we expected this, didn't we? Secondly, Wallace slept with me again last night."

"Did he talk to you?" I asked. "And could you feel him move?"

"No," she said, "he just snored all night. Apparently he generated some warmth because the bed was very warm and yet my electric blanket was turned off. I have invited Conrad to my room tonight to hear Wallace snore. 'Concerto in E Flat Minor,' we will call it. I'll phone you tomorrow morning and give you another report."

"Not quite so early tomorrow morning, Elizabeth," I begged. Nevertheless, at seven o'clock sharp, the telephone rang.

"What do you have going with Elizabeth?" muttered Dorothy, waking up out of a sound sleep. "This is the third morning she's called."

"Wish I knew," said I.

"Another interesting night, Richard," said Elizabeth. "You should see the strange, bewildered and quizzical expression Conrad is now wearing. At eleven last night, Wallace started snoring in my bed. Conrad was sitting in a chair next to the bed, reading his beloved *Wall Street Journal*. You should have seen his face! First alarm, then disbelief. Then a big smile as he got up and began to pull my bed apart."

" 'Okay, Liz,' he grinned, 'where's your tape recorder? You probably taped me when I was snoring and I'm hearing my own snores.' "

"But he couldn't find a tape recorder," said Elizabeth. "The big grin faded and was replaced by an anxious frown. 'Now, Liz,' he said, 'I've had enough. How are you making these snoring sounds?' "

" 'You'll have to ask Wallace,' " I told him.

"Conrad then got into my bed. 'Why have you got your blanket turned up so high?' he asked.

" 'It's off,' I told him, 'Look for yourself.'

" 'Crazy,' he said. 'And this snoring. The noise is coming from the bed. I don't understand this at all, Liz. I think I'd better call the police.'

" 'Nonsense,' I said. 'What are you going to tell them? Are you going to ask them to come out and arrest the invisible man who is snoring in my bed?' "

Well, Conrad finally shrugged off Elizabeth's Wallace. "It's very interesting," he told me later. "Still, you know the whole thing is impossible. I'm sure Liz and I were experiencing some kind of mutual hallucination." Shades of my psychiatrist friend!

Elizabeth reported that Wallace stayed with her for nearly two months, snoring in her bed every night. Even during the day she could feel his presence, which was warm and comforting. Then one day while she was working in her kitchen, the thought occurred to her that this companionship was really not a good thing to continue. So she said, "Wallace, it's time for you to leave me. Please go now, and please don't come back."

She said she felt Wallace leave immediately, and she was permeated with a wave of sadness and loneliness. But, nowadays, Elizabeth, always joyful and ebullient, tells everyone who will listen about her two months' day-and-night association wth Wallace.

The other day I overheard several of Elizabeth's acquaintances talking about her. "Poor Elizabeth," one of them said. "She has always been so bright. A Phi Beta and a graduate with honors from Reed, you know. But all this spook stuff she raves about. Obviously she is in desperate need of psychiatric treatment."

One day when Elizabeth and I were talking about Wallace, a flicker of skepticism must have crossed my face. She looked me firmly in the eye and said, "Richard, I swear on the soul of my dear departed mother, every word I have said is true. I have not embellished the truth and my imagination hasn't been working overtime either."

Recently I telephoned her to ask her permission to use her Wallace experience in this book. She was most enthusiastic but cautioned me not to use her real name, which of course I have not done.

Our phone conversation terminated with, "My fervent thanks to you, Richard, for arranging my attendance at the

Reiner seance. My Wallace experience was beautiful. Even though I no longer hear or feel his presence, I know he is watching over me. There is only one thing that perplexes me. Why did Wallace have to snore so loud?"

8

Fraud and a Hit

I didn't have good "vibes" about going to the Spiritualists' Camp Meeting, but my friend talked me into it anyway. I was intrigued when he said an internationally known physical medium would be there and we could watch him do materializations in an amber light. I had seen legitimate photographs of psychic fluid leaving the sensitive's body and forming into legs, arms, heads and other parts of the human body, but never had witnessed an actual materialization phenomenon. The admission fee was nominal, only $2 per person, claimed my friend.

As we went out the door, my wife's farewell remark was, "If you bring any spooks back with you, I'm going home to mother and this you had better believe!"

An hour later, I was one of about fifty people sitting around in a circle on a decrepit folding chair. We were in the gym of an old country schoolhouse and I was not happy! The admission fee was $5 not $2. The sitting was to last half an hour. Let's see, I mused, five times fifty, that's $250 for 30 minutes' work. Not bad! This fellow had better be good!

Besides being very uncomfortable, the ancient chair had something wrong with its folding mechanism. Every time I moved, it nipped my thigh. I complained to my friend and he offered to trade chairs—I declined, preferring martyrdom.

The medium, a man in his middle twenties and suffering from severe acne, sat on a creaky stool in the middle of the circle. He wore a crumpled brown tweed suit that didn't match his shiny, black patent-leather shoes. I noticed that his shoelaces, which seemed to be tied in a double bow, were brown. At least they matched his suit.

He explained that he would lecture for a quarter of an hour, then he would bring in our dear, departed relatives and friends who would give us messages of great importance.

The first part of his talk was interesting. He said, "Spiritualism began on March 31, 1848, when Margaret Fox asked her neighbors to come over and listen to the rapping noises that were occurring throughout the house when her two adolescent daughters were present. Soon, many other people found that they had mediumistic powers and could also produce rappings." He continued in an entertaining vein for a few more minutes, then embarked on a personal ego trip:

"I have appeared before the crowned heads in England and Europe and have brought enlightenment and contentment to thousands of people all over the world." As he continued his self-glorification, I attempted to get eye contact with him but was unsuccessful because he avoided looking at anyone directly by peering over their heads or at their feet.

The pull chain for the single light bulb was directly over his head. Abruptly he announced, as he reached for the chain, "I will now bring spirits into this room and will demonstrate my wonderful powers. This experience will forever live in your memories." The light clicked off and we were in total darkness.

"What about the amber light?" I asked.

"Oh, it was broken. . .I'll get another one tomorrow. Now I will go into trance and will materialize a loved one for some of you, and for others I will bring in your spirit guide. There was silence for a moment and then:

"Is there anyone in this room who is going abroad in the near future?"

I was the only one who answered yes.

"This is White Feather, your spirit guide, and I came to warn you to be careful when you are in France." The voice had a raspy growl like an old man but bore an unmistakable resemblance to the voice of the medium. In two weeks we were sailing to Australia, not France. This fraud is so crude it's an insult to our intelligence, I thought.

"Harold is here! Does anyone have a Harold in the spirit world?"

"My father's name was Harold!" a lady exclaimed.

"This is your dad, dear," a muffled voice said. "I'm very happy here in this wonderful spirit world. God bless you, daughter, and goodby."

"That didn't sound like father. He was born in Germany and spoke English with a decided accent. Furthermore, he never allowed any of us children to call him dad. . .it had to be father."

And so it went. The departed "loved ones" seemed to have suffered a deterioration of memory bordering on total amnesia, and their intellect appeared to have suffered a similar decline.

The half-hour "experience that would forever live in our memories" was almost over. I heard the alleged medium's stool creak. A few seconds later, close to my chair, a voice sounding like the medium holding his nose, said, "Remember, be careful in France and watch out for those pretty French girls!" At the same moment a frightful odor of unwashed feet assailed my nostrils. Even my friend in the next chair muttered, "Phew!"

The stool creaked again and the light went on. The medium was sitting on the stool with a self-satisfied smile on his face. I was not surprised to note that his shoelaces were untied. As I walked past him, I again smelled, more faintly this time, the rank odor of unclean feet.

My friend apologetically said, "I'm sorry, Dick, I didn't know. . . ." He was interrupted by a small, attractive, gray-haired lady who looked vaguely familiar. She handed me a sealed envelope and said, "Mr. Walker, we are not all frauds. Something unpleasant is going to happen to you tomorrow, and when it does, please read what's in this envelope." Before I could reply, she hurried out the door. To my friend I said,

"This is not my night and very likely tomorrow's not my day either because maybe that little lady is going to shoot me or something!" I stuck the envelope in my raincoat pocket and forgot about it.

My prediction for the next day was unhappily correct. No, the little lady didn't shoot me but it was almost as bad! I stepped off a curb and sprained my ankle. The sprain was so severe and swelled so rapidly that our family physician had to cut the sock off my foot. He said,

"I have never seen a worse sprain! You will be on crutches for at least two weeks."

"Impossible!" I replied. "I have to teach a dance class tomorrow night. All our teachers are busy so there is no one to substitute for me."

"Listen to me, Richard! You can't even put any weight on that foot. I'm sorry, but you will have to accept the fact that you are benched for two weeks."

This was disastrous news! The invitations to the classes had gone out and I had a family to feed.

As Dorothy was driving me home from the doctor's office, I wondered how that lady knew I was going to have an accident? I reached for the envelope in my pocket.

I opened the envelope, and on a piece of blue stationery was written, "For your ankle: Get the *Edgar Cayce Handbook for Health through Drugless Therapy*, by Reilly and Brod. Page 245. Read: Castor-Oil Packs, Directions." I was dumbfounded! Yet, she had made an accurate prediction so perhaps the treatment she recommended might work. It was worth a try. So, this desperate skeptic had his wife go to the book store and buy the book. Before retiring that night, I followed Edgar Cayce's directions explicitly. We soaked a wool flannel cloth in castor oil and wrapped it around the swollen ankle. We then applied a plastic cover over the flannel cloth to protect the bedclothes. Finally, we wrapped an electric heating pad around the ankle and turned it on to "medium."

The next morning when I got out of bed and was walking to the bathroom, I wondered what those oily cloths were doing around my ankle. Then I remembered! I removed the cloths and could scarcely believe what I saw! The ankle was still black and blue but there was no swelling. . . nor was there the slightest bit of pain—even when I deliberately twisted it! That night I taught the class without the smallest degree of difficulty.

I wish that little gray-haired lady would contact me because I want to thank her and also ask her some questions.

Needless to say, I am now an Edgar Cayce devoté. In the event you do not know, Edgar Cayce was a world-renowned clairvoyant who would go into a trance and give medical readings for the sick. His diagnoses were weirdly accurate and the treatments he prescribed were always effective. He was tested and examined by scientists from all over the world. To their bewilderment, he never failed a test even under the most rigorous conditions, and his medical theories proved to be totally correct. Thirty-six books and countless magazine articles have been written about this man, who was called the "sleeping prophet and medical telepathist of Virginia Beach."

One evening, I was enthusiastically extolling the therapeutic value of the magical castor bean to a group of my students. A doctor, who had been in earshot, sauntered up to me and admonished, "Practicing medicine without a license? Careful, Richard, you'll get into trouble!"

A little later, I noticed that he was unsuccessfully attempting to help a student with a dance step. I couldn't restrain myself. With a smile, I wandered over to him and said, "Practicing dance instruction without a license, doctor? Careful, you'll get into trouble."

9

Paranormal Episodes in Hawaii

About ten years ago, an old friend of mine—a retired Marine Corps officer—and his wife bought a 14-room house with 500 feet of ocean frontage on the island of Kauai, Hawaii, for $16,500. The adventures into the psychic world that occurred to these friends, the Masons, were so fascinating that I have related them to many friends.

Just for the fun of it, after telling about their fabulous buy, I would always ask, "Why do you think they got it so cheap?"

Most people would answer, "Termites?" Other guesses were "No plumbing," "Poor foundation," "Built on quicksand," "Couldn't get title insurance," and so on.

Finally someone would ask, "Was it haunted?"

"That's it!" I would exclaim. "It was indeed haunted."

After this statement, nearly seventy-five percent of my listeners would smile in disbelief and some would say, "Come, come, Richard, do you expect us to believe this?"

Before long, however, I would have an attentive audience. Often somebody would ask, "Where can I find reading material on this subject?"

Here is the story: Walter Mason and I had been close friends since we were both eleven years old. His wife, Eleanor, had achieved recognition in the field of education as a brilliant teacher of retarded children. Walt had been a construction engineer in the United States Marine Corps; and after retiring on the lovely island of Kauai, he accepted a job as consulting engineer at Mauna Loa Volcano Observation Center,* where a leading mainland university was engaged in a geological research program.

Incidentally, the Masons had never been at all interested in psychic matters. On several occasions I had attempted to engage them in conversations regarding psychic phenomena, but always without success. They were bright, open-minded people, yet in this area their minds were closed. Why spend time, they asked, in discussing a subject that is a hundred percent fraudulent?

Well, as the Masons tell their story, a few weeks after moving into their island dream home, they and their three toy poodles were relaxing in the family room. Walt and Eleanor were again congratulating themselves on their stupendous buy. Walt had taken a week's leave from his job in order to do some lawn work, and to complete a few small projects around the house per Eleanor's request.

They had purchased this property from Mr. and Mrs. Opuaa, an elderly native couple. The Opuaas had seemed very anxious to sell. At first they had asked $20,000, but they misinterpreted the surprised silence of the Masons, who had expected to pay at least twice that figure. The Opuaas quickly said, "All right, you can have it for $16,500." Walt

---

*Mauna Loa is the largest single mountain in the world. Its 10,000-cubic-mile mass is enough to cover the entire surface of the earth under a foot-thick layer of lava. In July, 1975, for seventeen hours, Mauna Loa expelled enough lava down its sides to pave a six-lane highway from New York to Portland, Oregon.

immediately wrote a check for earnest money, then retained a local attorney to draw up the final papers.

On the particular day when the story begins, Walt had finished building and installing shelves in the family room, and Eleanor had lovingly arranged her valuable collection of thirty-nine antique cups and saucers there.

Suddenly the Masons' three dogs started to whine.

"Look at them!" Eleanor exclaimed. "All three are staring at the same place in the middle of the carpet but there's nothing there."

The dogs were now backing up, tails between their legs, pitifully whining, still staring at that same place on the floor. "They see something we don't see," said Walt, "and they're absolutely terrified."

This was most unusual behavior for these dogs. The Masons had raised them from pups.

Yipping in terror, the dogs dashed from the room and scurried under the bed in one of the guest rooms. "What was all that about?" asked Eleanor.

"I don't know," said Walt, "though now I remember that when I asked Mr. Opuaa why he didn't have the home listed with a real estate agency, he said that realtors were not allowed to list houses like this. Remember that? I was so anxious to get the deal closed that what he said didn't seem important at the time. You don't suppose—"

Eleanor interrupted him. "Walt! Do you see what I see?"

Walt turned around and looked where Eleanor was looking. He gasped. "Your cup and saucer floating through the air . . . Good Lord!"

Walt had always been an irrepressible practical joker. "Walt," said Eleanor, her voice shaking, "if this is another of your practical jokes, I'm not amused. What have you done—tied fishing lines to my Dresden cup and saucer? You've gone too far this time!"

Face pale and eyes wide, Walt said, "I didn't do a thing. Oh, my God!"

The cup and saucer had been slowly floating in the air over to the side of the room where the carpet was not covering the floor. All at once they dropped and smashed.

Another cup, sitting on its saucer, left the shelf and floated dreamily through the air about six feet above the floor.

"Do something!" screamed Eleanor.

"I will," Walt muttered.

He leaped from his chair and started to stalk the cup and saucer. The valuable china pieces were moving very slowly toward the side of the room. About two inches away from them, Walt grabbed—but they shot out of his reach and crashed to the floor.

Two more cups and saucers floated from the shelves and started their flight to destruction. Eleanor ran sobbing from the room.

His jaws clenched, Walt tried time after time to grasp the floating china pieces but they seemed to have an intelligence of their own. His fingers would almost grab them, when they would dart out of his reach and crash.

Ten minutes later Eleanor returned with a neighbor couple she had summoned for help. There was Walter, sitting on the floor with perspiration and tears streaming down his face; and around the perimeter of the room lay the remains of thirty-nine valuable antique cups and saucers.

These neighbors had just moved in from the mainland the week before, and this was their introduction to the Masons. The husband turned to his wife and said, "We must be in the middle of a family fight. Look at this mess. They are either drunk or psychotic. Let's get out of here."

"No!" cried Eleanor, nearly hysterical. "We have been frightened—not fighting. My priceless cups and saucers have been flying through the air—and now look at them; they've all crashed on the floor!"

With a look of disgust, the neighbor wife said, "You really shouldn't drink in the daytime, my dear."

As their new neighbors marched out of the house, Eleanor joined Walter on the floor and they both wept.

That night there was little sleep. The three poodles, who usually slept in their own baskets in the family room, spent most of the night jumping nervously back and forth between Walt's bed and Eleanor's. Trembling and whining, the dogs would cock their heads at the same time and *listen*. What they heard apparently terrified them, because they would then try to burrow under the bodies of their owners.

The next morning, still crying and shaking, the dogs followed Eleanor into the family room. Again, the dogs' eyes were drawn to the same spot in the middle of the floor. Then they backed out of the room in haste, more disturbed than before. Walt and Eleanor looked after them.

"There's something there that we don't see," said Eleanor. "No, Walt—don't!"

But Walt walked to the center of the room and stomped his feet on the carpet. A puzzled look appeared on his face.

"What is it, Walt?" Eleanor asked. "What's the matter? Is something there?"

"There's a very cold breeze blowing on my feet. Come here, I want you to feel it too."

"No thank you," she said, backing away. "My feet are already cold."

Walt was now walking around on the floor. "Look," he said, "it's only this one spot, where the dogs were looking, that's cold. It's only about three feet across. What's going on here, Eleanor?"

10

Who's Turning on the Water?

After breakfast, Walt went outside to start some lawn work. Suddenly he heard water coming from a hose faucet a few feet behind him.

He whirled around. Water was pouring from the spigot. "Funny," he muttered. "I didn't turn that on. Some kid must have sneaked up and turned it on.—But where is he now? There's no place to hide."

Just as he turned off the water, Eleanor yelled from the house, "Walt! Get in here as fast as you can!"

"What now?" he thought. "Pots and pans flying through the air?"

He sprinted into the kitchen. There was Eleanor pointing a shaking finger at the faucet in the sink. Water was running out at full force.

"I didn't turn that on, Walter!" cried Eleanor. "It turned on by itself! I saw the handles turning right in front of my eyes! First the cold and then the hot!" She was interrupted by a sound from the bathroom next to the kitchen—the toilet in there was being flushed. They stared at one another.

Eleanor's voice shook. "Who's that in the bathroom now, Walter?"

"No one from this world," he muttered, heading for the bathroom. Sure enough, the toilet bowl was filling with water. But no one was in the bathroom.

Behind him he heard Eleanor cry, "Walt! Listen! The toilet is flushing now in the other bathroom!"

They ran to the other bathroom, adjacent to their bedroom. The water was emptying from the toilet bowl. Walt grasped the handle. It moved under his palm to flush again. With all his strength he tried to hold it. Then with a loud snap, something broke behind the handle.

Walt lifted off the porcelain tank cover. Maybe, he thought, he could stop the cycle. It was no use. He and this unseen force had broken something in the handle mechanism. No need to encourage further damage, at the price of plumbing repairs.

Suddenly water was running in the kitchen. "Not again," groaned Walter.

They dashed back to the kitchen. Both the hot and cold taps were on, and water was pouring out.

There was no opposition, however, from these handles as Walter turned them off. "Wonder why they wouldn't let me stop the toilet from flushing, yet I'm allowed to turn off the water here," he said.

Then he stared out the window. Water was pouring out of the two hose faucets in his line of vision.

He dashed outdoors and turned them off. Suddenly something warned him to check the two behind the house. They were on, too! All of the handles had been turned on as far as they would go.

As he turned them off, Eleanor shouted frantically from the house. "Walt! Walt! Everything is on! Water is running in both bathrooms and the toilets are being flushed and the water is on again in the kitchen!"

"Turn them all off!" he yelled. "I've got my hands full out here!" For the next two hours, the Masons turned off faucets, yet the moment they turned their backs, on would go the water again.

Finally, Eleanor called their water district and got the promise that a man would be out immediately. He did come at once, but when he arrived, all activity stopped. The Masons, embarrassed, expected disbelief and ridicule. To their surprise, the man said, "This has happened before, to other people."

He went on, matter-of-factly, "It looks like you may have to have this house exorcised. I can give you the name of a Kahuna priestess who lives on the other side of the island. Do you have a piece of paper handy? I'll write down her name and telephone number."

That night Walt and Eleanor heard loud rapping on the walls and ceiling of their bedroom. They had brought the dogs' baskets into the bedroom, but the dogs refused to stay in them. They were trembling and crying again.

"Well, we'll just have to move into one of the guest bedrooms," Walt said. Just as they were getting settled again, the rapping started on the walls and ceiling in there, even louder this time.

"All right," said Walt, "we'll sleep in the family room." This, too, was a mistake. As they were putting bedding on the hide-a-bed, the two large ashtrays on the coffee table flew through the air and crashed into the wall behind the hide-a-bed. And the knocking started again.

By now, the dogs were howling and urinating in great terror. "We've got to get out of here!" cried Eleanor. The rest of the night they spent in one of their cars, out in the garage.

It wasn't comfortable, but the dogs were quiet and there were no rapping noises.

Walt noted that the double garage was a recent addition to the property. Whether this had any significance, they did not know.

Next morning they returned to the house, where everything appeared normal. Even the dogs seemed normal, although when walking through the family room, all three would give that area in the middle of the floor a wide berth. And they still stared at it apprehensively.

Walt stood on the spot again. This time he could feel just a hint of cold breeze on his ankles, not at all as cold as before.

After breakfast, Eleanor opened the door of her sewing cabinet. Then she called out, "Walt! Look at this! All my needles are threaded. I never leave needles threaded!"

"Maybe you threaded them without realizing it," he said.

"That's impossible," she replied. "I tell you I never leave my needles threaded." She did the sewing she had planned, however, then removed the thread from all the needles. She stuck them into the cushion, which she placed back in the cabinet in the usual way.

That night, for a change, nothing happened to disturb the sleep which the Masons sorely needed. The dogs had also quieted down, although they were too nervous to stay in the family room. So Walt brought their sleeping baskets into the bedroom.

The next morning, feeling like a hunter stalking game, Eleanor opened the door of her sewing cabinet.

"I knew it!" she cried. "Look at this! All the needles are threaded again! Walt, I want you to install that extra padlock you've got out in the workshop on the cabinet door, and then bring the cabinet into our bedroom so we can watch it." Walt dutifully complied with his wife's request.

Except for one small incident with the dogs, that night also passed uneventfully. The one incident happened about midnight; Walt and Eleanor were awakened by the dogs howling in unison.

Walt snapped on his bed lamp. There were the dogs, staring in fear at the sewing cabinet which Walt had placed in the center of the room.

"See anything by the cabinet?" asked Eleanor.

"Not a thing," he answered. "But I doubt if I'm supposed to."

Whatever the dogs saw apparently left, because they soon lost interest, cuddled up, and went back to sleep. The following morning, Walt was abruptly awakened by a resounding slap on his back.

"Walt!" shouted Eleanor. "The key! It's gone!"

"What key?" he asked.

"The key to the padlock! I put it under my pillow last night before I went to sleep, and now it's gone! What did you do with it?"

"For heaven's sake, I didn't take the darned key," he said. "I didn't even see you put it under your pillow."

By now, the dogs were on Eleanor's bed, giving her morning greetings with their warm tongues. Cookie, the mother of the other two, wore a jeweled collar with a ring holding her metal rabies tag. Now, on the ring and next to the tag, Eleanor saw a key—the key to the lock on the sewing cabinet!

"Walter, just what is the big idea?" she asked. Don't tell me you did this in your sleep. Here." She tossed Cookie over onto Walt's bed. "I can't get the key off the ring."

Walt took off Cookie's collar and examined it. "No wonder," he said. "This key has been welded or fused to the ring. It will take a hacksaw to get it off. Eleanor, are you sure you put it under your pillow last night?"

"Of course I am—positive," she said.

"Well, let's unlock the cabinet and see about the needles," said Walt. Neither of the Masons was really surprised to find all the needles carefully threaded.

"What I don't understand," said Eleanor, "is that I didn't leave the spools of thread in the cabinet this time. I took them all out and left them in a drawer in the kitchen."

"Is that all you don't understand?" Walt asked dryly. He sawed the key from the ring, put it on his keychain with his other keys, and there it stayed from then on. And no more key problems developed.

For Eleanor, unthreading the needles became a game she never won. At night she would remove all the thread from the needles. In the morning Walt would unlock the padlock, and the needles would all be threaded. Their only clue to nocturnal activity in the cabinet was when the dogs would howl. Sometimes when this happened, Walt and Eleanor would turn on the lights and watch the dogs staring at the cabinet.

Once when this occurred, Eleanor asked Walt to look in the cabinet and see what was going on.

He countered with, "Oh no, thank you very much—they're your needles."

For several more days and nights, the pattern never varied. Then one morning the needles were not threaded. The Masons felt almost a little sad.

"Say, Eleanor," said Walt, "the dogs didn't wake us up once during the night. Guess our unseen guests must have gone."

"I hope so," she said. "Much more of this, and we'll have to find a dog psychiatrist for our little lambs."

"One for your big ram, too, I fear," said Walter.

Things gradually began to get pretty much back to normal in the Mason household—that is, except for the dogs, who still were not at ease in the family room. They would often huddle together and stare apprehensively at that area in the middle of the room. There always appeared to be something there that only they could see.

One afternoon, Walter called from the front door, "Eleanor, will you please take the dogs out to the backyard before I come in? I picked up a nice, gentle cat out in the road, and I want to bring her into the family room to see how she reacts."

When the dogs were put outside, Walt walked into the family room, with the purring cat in his arms. Abruptly, the purring stopped. The cat's body stiffened.

"Probably smells the dogs," said Walt. "Oh-oh, the cat is staring transfixed at the same spot that frightens the dogs."

Suddenly the cat gave an unearthly shriek and sank her claws into Walt's arm. She traveled up his shoulder, leaped to an open window ledge and disappeared, still shrieking.

Eleanor ran into the room. "What did you do to that poor cat? I've never heard a sound like that come out of a cat before."

"I didn't do a thing to her," said Walt. "I just showed her the dogs' spooky spot on the rug, and did she get upset! Look at my arm! Will you please get some alcohol for it?"

Eleanor went to get the medication, and Walt walked over to the suspect area on the carpet.

No cold breeze on my feet now, he mused—but he spoke too soon!

This time the breeze on his ankles was exceptionally cold.

11

The Last Straw

The next day Walt had to get up early. After a week's vacation he was going back to work at the Research Center, so it would be a good idea to get to bed early. He said goodnight to Eleanor and the dogs, who were watching TV in the family room. He closed the bedroom door, got into bed and turned out his light.

Because at this time the Masons didn't have air-conditioning in the house, they left the windows open at night and slept with only a sheet for cover. Walt was just drifting off when the sheet was violently pulled from his bed.

Was Eleanor now becoming a practical joker? He looked toward the door. It was still closed. He turned on his light. The sheet was lying on the floor at the foot of the bed.

One of the dogs must have pulled it off, he thought, glancing over at the dogs' baskets. Then he remembered that the dogs were in the family room with Eleanor, watching TV. Eleanor's bed was untouched. It was perfectly obvious that no one else was in the room.

Nevertheless, Walt looked under both beds: he even checked the closet. Nothing was visible anywhere—he hadn't really expected otherwise. Then he got back into bed and pulled the sheet up. He could dimly hear the sounds of the TV through the closed door.

Guess I'll leave the light on for a while, he thought, closing his eyes and starting to relax. He was just getting sleepy when—Snap! The sheet was again snatched off violently. This was too much! He had put up with all that other stuff without too much complaint, but having his sheet jerked off when he needed his sleep—that was another matter.

Again he pulled the sheet back up. This time he was going to be ready!

With muscles tensed he waited. When the sheet left his body again, his arms flailed wildly. But they flailed the air. There was nothing there. His powerful blows came in contact with nothing at all.

He pulled the sheet off the floor and covered himself again.

Okay, he decided grimly, if the sheet left the bed again, he was leaving with it. And he tightly clenched the sheet with both hands.

He didn't have long to wait. "Wow!" he yelled as he was jerked up nearly to a standing position. And it was not Walt that let go this time, but the sheet, split across from side to side.

Walt's yell brought Eleanor running, but not the dogs. They remained back in the family room, now howling in close harmony.

When Walt explained what had happened to one of her brand-new sheets, Eleanor said, "Well, this is the last straw. We're going to hire that Kahuna priestess to exorcise this house. What did you do with her phone number?"

"It's in my wallet," he said. "But wait a minute," he added. "I've got another idea first. Tomorrow at the Center I'll tell some of the scientists what's been happening to us. Perhaps they'll have some suggestions."

The rest of the night passed without further incident, although the dogs were trembling again, and refused to sleep in their baskets. To quiet their whining, Eleanor let them sleep on her bed.

12

There Is a Natural Explanation

At lunch the following day, with three American scientists who were doing research at the Volcano Observation Center, Walter related in detail the disturbing psychic events that had been occurring.

The three men listened attentively and with apparently considerable interest. Then Dr. Germaine said, "That was an interesting story, Walter, and I believe it bears investigation. However, I assure you a natural explanation will be forthcoming. Several things are possible, such as earth movement under the house, or an unusually strong electromagnetic field in your area. I firmly believe, also, that something is causing you and your wife to hallucinate."

"Do dogs hallucinate also?" asked Walter.

"Well, I don't believe so, but you see, when you and your wife are hallucinating, you are only imagining that the dogs have developed peculiar behavioristic patterns," said Dr. Germaine.

Dr. Merriman spoke up. "I would be interested in taking some sensitive instruments to your house for an investigation.

We can monitor and record whatever unusual forces are operating there, and as Bill Germaine said, we will disclose a natural explanation."

The third scientist said, "Count me out. I have better things to do with my spare time than investigating mental aberrations."

"Thank you for your interest in our little problem, gentlemen," said Walt. "Will you join us for dinner at our house next Saturday evening at eight? And then, if you will also spend the night with us, perhaps on Sunday morning you can activate your instruments. After that we will go to the country club for lunch, and wind up the day shooting nine holes."

"Agreed," said Dr. Germaine. "How about you, Steve? Are you free?"

"Yep," said Merriman. "I have no commitments for the weekend. Count me in."

The third scientist said dourly, "What a waste of time. Count me out."

Walt, with relief in his heart, said, "Thank you, fellows! I'll barbecue steaks, and Eleanor makes a mean Mai Tai."

The rest of the week passed without further disturbances at the Masons'. Whatever forces had been at work seemed to have declared a psychic moratorium. On Saturday evening, the two scientists promptly arrived at the Masons' villa, laden down with cases of instruments, golf clubs, and overnight bags.

Eleanor showed the men to their rooms and then went back to the kitchen to complete dinner preparations. Walt was on his way outside to start the barbecue when a yell from the bathroom stopped him in his tracks.

Steve Merriman opened the bathroom door, looking rather startled, but he grinned when he saw Walter.

"Walt, we're getting a little action. I was just about to turn on the water to wash my hands, and I'll be damned if the handle didn't turn on by itself—full force, too! Strange plumbing you have here. Do you have some wrenches? I would like to examine the mechanism thoroughly."

Bill Germaine had now joined them, chuckling. "Steve, are you sure you didn't imagine the water turned on by itself? Walt has been telling us a lot of strange stories, and you know the power of suggestion."

Walt produced the wrenches, and Steve proceeded to disassemble the basic fixture in the bathroom, while Bill continued to kid him.

"Nothing wrong," Steve said at last. "Everything is perfectly normal here. I thought Walt had hooked up a remote-control device which could turn on the water at his wish, from some other place in the house. Apparently, though, he hasn't."

After reassembling the fixture, they were called into the family room by Eleanor, for Mai Tais.

"Where do you feel that cold breeze on the floor, Walt?" asked Steve.

"Right over here. I'm standing on it. Come on over. I think you'll feel it too." Steve and Bill walked over to Walt.

"Yes, indeed, it is cool here," said Steve. "You must have an air-conditioning duct aimed at this area on the floor."

"I told you," said Walt, "we don't have any air-conditioning in the house, yet."

"You must be kidding," said Bill, and both men walked around the room looking for the duct.

"Fellows, I have not been kidding you. Everything I've told you is the gospel truth. Now, if you'll excuse me, I must get out there and start the steaks."

When Walt and Eleanor had left the room, Steve said, "What do you think, Bill? Some of the boys at work say that Walt is quite a practical joker."

"I'll reserve judgment until later," Bill replied. "Let's get a thermometer on the floor, and there's a plug-in for the seismograph."

The second the thermometer was placed on the floor, the mercury dropped from 83° to 45°. "Impossible for such a rapid drop," said Steve, puzzled. "Obviously this is a defective instrument."

"Is the tube broken?" asked Bill

"No."

"Well, then, how can it be defective?" asked Bill. "Hey! Look at that seismograph! Do you feel any movement? According to the reading, we are experiencing an earthquake of 7.9 magnitude."

"There is no earth movement," said Steve. "We must have defective equipment."

"That's imposssible. I had all these instruments checked yesterday," Bill declared. "There is nothing wrong with them. Oh, my! Look at that thermometer! It's down to 37 Farenheit now!"

"Has the seismograph changed, too?"

"Yep! It's up to 8.5! I don't understand this at all," said Bill. "But there just has to be a natural explanation."

"I hope those won't be famous last words, Bill. Just wait until the handle on the water faucet beats you to the draw! Let's set up the other equipment. Hope we don't blow a fuse!"

They plugged in the instrument for measuring quantity of magnetic waves. Then they set up a battery-operated Geiger counter capable of measuring up to 10,000 roentgen rays.

Bill took a look at the Geiger counter and gasped. "Good Lord, Steve, anyone who has been in that six-square-foot cold area is dead!"

Steve stared. "Then we're dead, and so are the Masons. We've all stood there."

"Just a minute, though," said Bill, trying to keep calm. "Let's not get panicky. I think our equipment is being hoaxed by something we don't understand just yet. Let's pull everything out of the suspect area, and set them up in another part of the room."

"Too hot a spot for me," said Steve. "I'm not going in there after them. Here, we'll push them out with this chair."

Set up in the new area, all the instruments now registered normal. Geiger counter, zero. Magnetometer, zero. Seismograph, zero. And thermometer, 83°.

"Okay," said Bill. "Now let's put them back where they were."

With the chair, they shoved the instruments back into the suspect area. Immediately the needles on the Geiger counter and the magnetometer jumped to the highest points on their scales. The thermometer dropped to 54° Fahrenheit, and the seismograph rose to 8.5.

At this point, Walter walked into the room, announcing that dinner would be served out on the lawn. Then he looked at the two men. "Say, you both appear sort of pale. Bill, what are you shaking for?"

"We've got bad news for you, Walter," said Steve. "We have all stood in that suspect area, and felt the cold breezes which are blowing from east to west but apparently not coming from anywhere. Well, the Geiger shows ten thousand roentgen rays of radiation in that six-square-foot area. It is very likely that none of us will be alive in the morning."

"Don't tell Eleanor," said Walt. "I believe she can't take much more of this. Wait a minute, though! Both Eleanor and I have stood over there several times, and felt the cold air on our feet. If radiation is there, how come we're still alive?"

"I don't know," said Steve. "I suppose it's possible, though, that some other forces are influencing the instruments. But it's really not likely. There must be a natural explanation."

"Well," said Walt, "if there is going to be a last supper, it's going to be a cold one if we don't get out there now and eat it."

Individual tables had been prepared on the lawn overlooking the ocean, where Eleanor was waiting. "Why so gloomy, gentlemen?" she greeted them. "You look like the world's coming to an end."

Under his breath, Bill remarked, "It may be, for us."

"Sit down and drink your Mai Tai while Walt gets the steaks from the barbecue," said Eleanor. She had placed each drink in a plastic holder, fastened to an arm of each chair.

Steve sat down and reached for his glass. As his fingers touched it, it flew out of his hand, sailed through the air, missed Bill's head by not more than an inch, and shattered on the ground about 30 feet away.

"Why did you do that?" Bill exclaimed.

"I didn't!" Steve protested. "It flew out of my hand with terrific force. I had nothing to do with it. I just barely touched it."

"I'll get you another," said Eleanor. "Drinking utensils, especially valuable ones, appear to be expendable around here," she added dryly.

Dinner was not disturbed by further events. Afterward the men went back into the family room to check the equipment. Eleanor carried the dinner dishes back to the kitchen, closely followed by the three dogs—which suddenly began to tremble again.

In the family room, Walt walked toward the instruments.

"Stop!" yelled Steve. "Don't go in there! It's dangerous. Please don't go any closer, Walt. See, just as before, all the instruments are registering maximum. Look at that seismograph! It's registering now as high as it will go—9 on the Richter scale."

"All right now, let's get them out of there," Bill said in a strained voice. "No, Walt, we'll push them out with that chair. Don't go in there."

"If that Geiger counter is reading accurately, didn't you say we've already had it?" Walt asked. He unplugged two of the instruments, pulled them and the Geiger counter off the floor, and placed them in their carrying cases.

"Yes," Bill agreed. "There's no need for medical help, if we've taken what I think we have. But I don't understand it. By this time all of us should be violently nauseated, and even semi-comatose. Yet we're not. Walter, will you please bring in the dogs, so we can observe their reactions at first hand?"

Walt went after the dogs, and Steve sank into a chair, holding his head in his hands. "I have a terrible headache, anyway," he said. "I hope it isn't a symptom of radiation poisoning."

"Well, I feel fine, strangely enough," said Bill. "Ah, here comes Walt with the dogs."

Walt came in with the three poodles in his arms. At once they started whining pitifully, their eyes riveted to the area on the floor where the instruments had been.

"Those dogs," Bill declared, "certainly see something we do not see."

As Walter walked closer to the area, the three dogs in his arms yelped in terror and started urinating. Walter backed away, putting the dogs down on the floor. They fled yelping from the room, eyes wide with fright.

"This headache of mine says I must go to bed," said Steve. "We'll do a little more investigating in the morning—if there will be a morning for us."

"I'm ready for bed, too," said Bill. "See you all in the morning—God willing."

Bill and Steve were occupying the two guest bedrooms that were directly across the hall from the Masons' master bedroom. At about two o'clock the next morning, Walt and Eleanor were awakened by loud voices, clearly audible through the open doorways.

"Steve, I tell you this noise is being produced on the external surface of this paneling!"

"Impossible, Bill! There's nothing here in the room that can produce these knocks!"

Then loud raps began coming from both guest rooms. "Now they're getting the treatment," Walt whispered to Eleanor, who was kneeling by the dogs' baskets, attempting to quiet them.

They heard Steve say, "Let's get the instruments and set them up in here."

"No," said Bill. "The results would just upset us still more. You know we can't get an accurate reading in this house. And I can't sleep with all this racket. How's your head?"

"Hm, that's funny," said Steve. "It's okay now."

"Any nausea?"

"None."

"You know, Steve, if we had taken that much, we wouldn't be talking now."

"I know."

"What do you think?"

"I'm stupefied."

"I'll share that thought with you."

Suddenly the rapping in both rooms ceased. "I guess we're going to be allowed to go back to bed," Bill said cautiously.

"Goodnight, Steve."

"Goodnight," came Steve's voice.

Later on, the Masons were again awakened, this time by a car pulling out of their driveway. Walt turned on the light, got up, and looked into the guest rooms. They were empty.

"It's not like those fellows to sneak away in the middle of the night," he told Eleanor, "without a word of explanation or thanks."

He went into the kitchen. A note lay on the table by the back door. He read:

> "Thanks for your hospitality. Eleanor, your cuisine was superb and your flying Mai Tais out of this world, which brings us to our final conclusion. There must be a natural explanation, but we don't know what it is. We have two suggestions to resolve your problems. Call that Kahuna priestess for help and/or sell this house at any price and move out, promptly. With warm personal regards.
>
> Bill and Steve
>
> P.S.: Steve's headache came back. We both have developed a sudden, overwhelming longing for our own quiet habitats. Raincheck on the golf game."

Back in their bedroom, Walt handed Eleanor the note, sighing deeply. "I don't know what will happen to me if I don't get some uninterrupted sleep pretty soon. Goodnight, Eleanor."

Sleep had just arrived when the rapping started in their room, very loud this time. Everywhere. On the walls, ceiling, floor, nightstands, dressers, chairs. The dogs were now howling.

Walt said, "You win, whoever you are. Come on, Eleanor, bring the dogs. We're off for the garage."

13

Exorcism—Hawaiian Style

First thing in the morning, Walter made the phone call to the Kahuna priestess.

"Can you come right away?" he asked. "You don't have transportation? Yes, I'll pick you up. It will take me about an hour to get there. You live right next to... yes, I know where that is. Uh, what do you charge? Ten dollars? All right. What? Wait just a minute, please, let me write that down. All right—you want me to buy twelve ounces of corn... two pounds of rice... Hawaiian salt, all right... one-fifth of Canadian Club—does it have to be Canadian Club? All right. Oh, brown rice? All right. Shrimp? How much? One and one-half pounds. Coconut milk? From three coconuts. Okay. And what? What did you say? Two dead mongooses? Where would I get two dead mongooses? You will get them? Good. You get the mongooses. Yes, I'll pay the five dollars for them. Is that all? Fine. All right, then, I'll pick you up there in an hour."

"Well, Eleanor," said Walt, "this is out last hope. See you in a couple of hours."

After buying the items the priestess had ordered, Walt drove to the village where she lived. He found her small house without difficulty and knocked on the door. A tiny, toothless, elderly native woman, holding a burlap sack, opened the door.

"You Mr. Mason? Gimme five dollars now. I got mongooses." She lifted the sack with a triumphant smile.

Walt took a five- and a ten-dollar bill out of his wallet and offered them to her.

"No, I only take a five. You gimme the ten when I feenish."

Hm, thought Walt, a lady of principle.

On the way back, the old lady was not very talkative, although she volunteered some information. It would be nice if they had a blender, she said, because she was going to mix together all of the ingredients, including the two mongooses. Then she would chant certain words as she threw the mixture out of the windows and doors.

This was going to be an aboriginal exorcism rite, pure and simple, thought Walt.

The ceremony, said the old lady, would take all night long, and the Masons and their dogs must leave the house. Walt said that would be fine with them; they were getting used to sleeping in the garage anyway.

But that wouldn't do, she said. "No, you gotta go five miles away from da house."

Oh-oh, thought Walt. This is getting more and more expensive. A motel bill, the good booze going out the window, plus all that other stuff I bought. Five bucks to the old lady for the two dead mongooses. And we'll have to get a new blender—Eleanor will never use the old one again, after the mongoose dissolution. Steaks and drinks for Bill and Steve, and they might need psychiatric treatment, for which they will very likely send me the bill. And the dogs certainly need psychiatric help. And so will Eleanor and I, if this exorcism doesn't work.

That night the Masons and their canine family stayed at the Kanuai Hilton, a motel more than five miles away from their house. In the office they saw a sign—*No Pets Allowed.*

After swearing the dogs to silence, Eleanor put them into an airline travel bag, with a towel over their heads, and sneaked them into the room. Then, in desperate need of sleep, the Mason family of five collapsed on the king-sized bed, where they remained in blessed oblivion until the following morning.

But in the morning as they were leaving the room, Cokie, the elder son of Cookie, poked his head out from under the concealing towel and barked at one of the maids. The girl gave the Masons an accusing glare and rushed away—no doubt straight to the office—to report the Masons' heinous infraction.

As Walt and Eleanor, with all three dogs now barking joyfully from inside the travel bag, rushed out to their car, Walt said, "More trouble. Now we will be on record, along with thieves who steal towels and ashtrays. We'll never dare come back here again. Well, there's one consolation, I paid for the room last night. I'd hate to face the manager this morning."

When they arrived home, the old lady met them at the back door. With her toothless smile she announced, "It okay now. I got it fixed. They no come back for a long time. You pay ten dollar now."

A not-too-pleasant odor assailed Eleanor's nostrils, and she saw patches of the exorcism fluid by the door and under the kitchen window.

"Walter, do clean that stuff up. I can't stand that awful smell."

The Kahuna priestess' smile disappeared. "No!" she cried. "Don't touch! It gotta stay there for whole day. It maybe smell but no draw flies!"

She was right, the flies did not come. Nor did the spirits—or whatever they were—return, except once.

About five years later, a small bit of action started again, but this was my fault. I will explain in a later chapter.

14

No-Blessing Courts Disaster

A life insurance policy on my wife, Dorothy, had matured, producing extra cash. At the same time, a letter from the Masons in Hawaii arrived, urging us to bring the kids and come to visit them for a couple of weeks on Kauai.

Walt had written to me in great detail about their "haunted house" experiences. Now I was eager to get the facts first hand, and of course, to spend some time with my dear old friends. Dorothy, Lynn, and John were also eager for a sun break, and the kids had never been to Hawaii. So away we flew.

But to descend on the Masons for two weeks with a couple of teenage children might strain a wonderful friendship. So, we spent a week in Waikiki, then one week on Kauai with Walt and Eleanor. Later, I'll return to our week in Waikiki and relate two occurrences pertinent to the subject of this book. But now back to Kauai.

The Masons greeted us warmly at the airport, with beautiful leis of fresh orchids and plumeria. They had brought both cars in order to handle all our bodies and luggage.

On the drive to their house, son John and I were riding with Walt in his small but sprightly Fiat. He said, "Dick, this car is yours for as long as you stay with us. You will recall I wrote to you that I finished my work at the Volcano Research Center. Now I'm starting to build a guest cottage on our lot, right next to the water.

"Incidentally," he went on, "before I poured the foundation, I had the property blessed, and by the same little old lady who got rid of our problems for us, five years ago. She only charged me three dollars, plus a package of cigarettes, and it took her about two minutes. She chanted some words in Hawaiian with both arms raised in the air, sort of like a minister giving an invocation. It's a mighty cheap insurance policy." Walt smiled and shook his head, evidently remembering what he and Eleanor had been through when they first bought the property.

"Do you know," he continued, "before any kind of structure is built anywhere in the Islands—a high-rise apartment, a condominium, office building, school, private home, government building—anything at all—the property is first blessed by a Kahuna priest or priestess. Builders had to learn that, the hard way. Not too long ago, for instance, a contractor started a condominium without having the property blessed.

"Now you may believe this or not, but before the framing crew had finished, two of the workers were dead—freak accidents that never should have happened. Then, for no apparent reason, a beautiful pour of five thousand square feet of concrete slab cracked, as if water had got under it, though tests proved later that this had not happened. *And then*—the contractor himself, a healthy man in his early thirties, died of a heart attack!

"Well, the owner got the message at last. He had the framing torn down and the foundation and slab broken up and taken away. Then he started all over again. But this time the property was blessed, and the structure was completed with no further problems." Walt smiled, marvelling.

"Similar disasters have occurred, time after time," he recalled, "throughout the whole Hawaiian island group. No one in his right mind would start building anything here, no matter whether it's a dog-house or a $5 million government building, without first having the property blessed. Furthermore. . . ."

I just had to interrupt. "Speaking of government buildings, Walt, last week we took the Pearl Harbor tour in a Navy launch. It was easy to see the stack of the *Arizona* sticking up out of the water like a tombstone for all those hundreds of boys whose bodies are still down there in that sunken ship . . . but back to the subject of blessing. The tour director on the launch was an ensign in uniform and he told us a most fascinating story. Maybe you know it?

"He said that some years ago, the Navy started to construct a multimillion-dollar submarine shed—even though they had been warned not to build in the selected area because it was in the sacred waters of the great white shark. However, if they felt they had to build right there, they were advised to be sure and have the area properly blessed, in order to avoid a great catastrophe.

"Well, the area was not blessed and the construction was started. By the time it was finished, it had taken five times longer than it was supposed to. Then, instead of five million dollars, it cost thirty million—and this was in the days when inflation was not a factor. Further, more than three hundred workers died in construction accidents, though this project shouldn't have cost any lives. And get this!—when the day finally arrived for the dedication ceremony, the entire structure collapsed!

"Divers were sent down to find the cause of the catastrophe. To their amazement, in the huge concrete foundation they found the imprint of a great white shark. That was a costly lesson for the United States Navy, the ensign told us, and one that would not be repeated. From that time on, funds have been allocated for blessing any structural project, by proper persons of Kahuna, prior to the start of construction."

"Yes," Walt said, "I've heard this story before, and I'm sure it's true."

"There is one other incident I'd like to tell you about, Walt," I said. "We've been corresponding with a native-born Hawaiian couple we met a couple of years of ago while on a cruise to Australia. He's the manager of one of the large stores at Alamawana—if I'm pronouncing that right—Shopping Mall, and she teaches commercial art at the University of Hawaii. They took us out to dinner last week and then to the Barefoot Bar for further fellowship.

"Since I know very little about Kahuna, I was curious to learn more. I was sure that Howard and his wife, being Hawaiian-born, would be knowledgeable on the subject. I asked him if he would tell us about what must be their old-time religion—Kahuna.

"Howard smiled a thin little smile. 'Sorry, Dick,' he said, 'but this is a subject we don't discuss with *haole*,* even good friends like you.'

"This remark discouraged me only momentarily. By this time, Dorothy was kicking me under the table, but I persisted. 'Please, Howard, just give me a thumbnail sketch on Kahuna.'

" 'No,' he replied.

"I could see that our lovely friends were upset, and knew I should have dropped the subject. Another of my wife's

---

*Foreigner.

'Please shut up' kicks on my shin just seemed to egg me on. 'Oh, come on, Howard,' I urged him, 'tell us only a couple of incidents, and I won't press you further.'

"He sighed. 'All right, Dick, but I will appreciate it if you will curb your laughter—and when I'm finished, please, no further questions.'

" 'Agreed,' I said.

"So Howard began. 'When my wife and I were young, our transportation was horse-and-buggy. Usually, on Saturday nights, we would go to a dance, which was probably like your grange hall dances. Frequently, on the way home, evil spirits, which looked like meteors, would follow us at treetop height. This was not good, so to destroy them we would shout swear words at them, and they would explode like Roman candles and disappear.

" 'On several occasions, when we left the dance hall, a small black Mina bird would be flying directly over us. We knew this was a bad spirit that we could not destroy, so I would whip up the horse to make him gallop. However, by the time we got home, that bird would be as large as the buggy we were riding in! I am not exaggerating and our imaginations were not working overtime.' (My wife and I could see that Howard meant every word.)

" 'Every native-born Hawaiian,' Howard continued, 'has a protective spirit who watches over him. For example, I do a great deal of skindiving, which is my hobby, and my protective spirit is a very large shark that is with me whenever I'm in the water. I can identify him by his huge size, and by a crescent-shaped scar under his left dorsal fin. I have been in waters where no other human being could survive, because of man-eating sharks and other deadly marine life. Yet I am in no danger because my protecting shark is always with me. Now this is all I'm going to tell you, Dick,' he finished. 'The subject is closed.' "

Walt, who had seemed mildly interested in this story, agreed. "We have several Hawaiian friends," he said, "and they will not discuss Kahuna with us. If you wanted to keep Howard and his wife as friends, Dick, I think you made a mistake to pressure them as you did."

"I'm afraid you're right, Walt. Even though I apologized as they drove us back to our apartment, we noted a lack of cordiality in their conversation. When they said goodby, it sounded final."

And final it was. When we returned home, I wrote Howard and his wife a thank-you letter, and also invited them to be our house guests whenever they came to the mainland. But we never heard from them again. My persistence had lost us two wonderful friends.

15

I Experiment Again—Briefly

The Masons settled us comfortably in their beautiful ocean-front home. John had the hide-a-bed in the family room, and Lynn her own bedroom. Dorothy and I were given the largest guest bedroom. We were all anticipating a grand week of sunning, swimming, beachcombing, golfing, and, of course, fellowship with our old friends, Walt and Eleanor.

My Scotch ancestors must have been smiling, too, because unlike our first week, at Waikiki, this week was going to be very inexpensive.

But I almost blew it. Against my wife's wishes, I had brought along my Ouija board. At home the board had produced some amazing phenomena, which I will discuss later in this book. I reasoned that there on Kauai in a location where there had been considerable psychic activity, such as had happened at the Masons' home, perhaps the Ouija board would produce some unusual action.

After dinner, the first evening, I produced said board and asked Eleanor if she would play it with me. She frowned briefly, but then gave me her usual warm smile and said, "Why, yes, Richard, if you want to. It will be my pleasure."

The planchette didn't need its usual warming-up period. It immediately darted from letter to letter, son John writing down the words that were spelled. The first question I asked was, "Are there any discarnates in this room at the present time?" The planchette moved rapidly to *yes*.

"Is there any way you can let us know of your presence?" I asked.

Many, it spelled out.

"Please tell us," I requested.

It answered, *Take Kakie to Lynn's bedroom, put her on the bed, and watch her.* Kakie, by the way, is the youngest poodle.

We all trooped into Lynn's room. Eleanor placed Kakie in the middle of the bed and sat down at the head while Lynn sat at the foot. The rest of us remained standing, waiting for whatever might happen next. Meanwhile, Kakie, wagging her tail, looked adoringly at her mistress, Eleanor.

Suddenly the dog acted as if a firecracker had exploded under her. With an agonized yelp she jumped at least two feet straight up in the air. Her eyes bulging with fright, she looked at the place on the bed where she had just been sitting, jumped into Eleanor's arms, looked back at the place on the bed, then tried to burrow deeper into Eleanor's protecting arms.

There was no mistake. The dog saw something which we could not see and she was absolutely terrified.

The dog was not the only one disturbed. That old familiar chill crept up my spine. Lynn screamed and ran out of the room. John said, "Oh, my God," and slowly backed out of the room after her.

I quickly regained my own composure and said cheerfully, "Come on, Eleanor, let's go back to the Ouija board." Then I saw the expression on Eleanor's face and knew there would be no more Ouija-boarding in her home. At that point, Dorothy made a statement that instantly wiped the smiles off the faces of my Scotch ancestors.

"Richard," she said, "if you don't stop your experimenting, immediately, the children and I will go to the Kauai Hilton for the rest of the week. And this will cost you at least forty dollars per night."

I knew when I was stopped. "Okay, okay, you win," I replied. So I didn't lose money, but I did lose a lot of sleep for the rest of that week. Since Lynn refused to set foot in her bedroom, she of course had to sleep with us. And it was only an old-fashioned double-bed—not even queen-sized.

Just as I was about to slip into dreamland that first night, I heard a thin voice say, "I'm a little nervous out there in the family room, so I guess I'll sleep with you."

Well, could I turn down my sixteen-year-old son? Of course not. Now we were four in a bed for two.

The rest of my family seemed to have no problem getting to sleep, but not I. Obviously there was no room in the bed, to toss and turn, so I tried the floor for a while. But that was no good at all.

At last a brilliant thought came to me. Why not sleep in John's hide-a-bed in the family room! This I did.

First, though, I stood in the suspect spot, in the middle of the floor, which had caused such a lot of trouble for the Masons. I knew what to expect, because I had felt cold air on my ankles in the Reiners' seance room. But here, there was no cool breeze. Darn it!

I lay awake for some time, hoping to hear a few raps. None occurred. Before I fell asleep, my final thought was to wish I wasn't so hooked on the subject. Probably I had brought misery to several nice people that evening, even a sweet little poodle."

The poodle must have forgiven me, because early the next morning I awoke having difficulty breathing. Kakie was lying on my face. When I gently moved her to my pillow, she smiled and licked my Roman nose. No question about it, I was forgiven.

16

The Ouija Board

Ouija—from the French *oui* and the German *ja*, both meaning *yes*.

The Ouija board appears to be a method of releasing the subconscious. Perhaps it is also a means of communication between the living and the dead.

This board can be purchased in various sizes with the average being about 20 inches long and 14 inches wide. Printed on the face of the Ouija board are the letters of the alphabet in two rows of large capitals. The word *Yes* appears in the upper left-hand corner of the board, and the word *No* in the upper right-hand corner. Beneath the alphabet are the numerals 1 2 3 4 5 6 7 8 9 0. At the bottom of the board is the word *Goodby*. A small pointer or planchette is provided with the board. The pointer looks like a three-legged miniature table, triangular in shape.

To operate the Ouija board, two persons (usually) place their fingertips lightly on the pointer, which is resting on the board. Often you may have to wait several minutes before the pointer starts to move. When it does start, let your fingers go with it. Don't press down, and of course don't try to stop the movement. You will swear that the other person is voluntarily moving the pointer with his fingers. At the same time he is convinced that you are consciously moving it.

At first, the pointer will often indicate letters that add up to gibberish. The standard opening question is, "Is there anyone here?" The pointer will probably glide to the word *Yes*. Now ask the personality who is answering to spell out its name, which it usually does promptly. Ask for the place and time of birth and death. Ask for the names of other members of the personality's family, and whether they are living or dead. If the answer is that they are dead, ask when and where they died.

When working the Ouija board, you or your partner should write down the questions and answers, either when the pointer stops between messages, or when it just pauses, as it often does. Better yet, if possible, have a third person help you by writing down the questions and answers for you. And rather than continually using the question-and-answer procedure, occasionally just sit quietly with your fingertips resting lightly on the pointer. Soon the pointer will spell out its own message to you without being prompted by any query from you.

Perhaps the best-known case of a Ouija-board message was the remarkable performance of a housewife, Mrs. Pearl Curran. Mrs. Curran lived in St. Louis, Missouri. One day in the summer of 1913, Mrs. Curran was operating the board by herself, as a parlor diversion. After a while, the pointer started spelling out a message from a female personality who claimed to be the spirit of an English spinster in the 17th century, a certain Patience Worth.

From then on, over a period of the next twenty-five years, Patience Worth dictated, through Mrs. Curran, an intimate account of life in Elizabethan England. She followed this up with a number of novels, set in even earlier historical periods, including a description of life in Jerusalem at the time of the Crucifixion. A considerable amount of poetry with a 17th-century flavor also came through. All of this extensive material was published, and it was appraised very favorably by literary critics.

Mrs. Curran, though, had never been out of her home state of Missouri! Nor was she interested in history. Moreover, she was not an educated woman, and her personality was nothing like Patience Worth's. Yet, with Patience Worth working through her hands, Mrs. Curran wrote in the idiom of the 17th century, and with the archaic spelling of the time. In her novels she spoke of daily household articles which had long since vanished from memory.

Though the Patience Worth case was thoroughly investigated by experts, no hint of fraud was ever discovered. Spiritualists accept that Patience Worth actually was what she claimed she was. Other people, however, have suggested that Mrs. Curran, entirely without her own conscious knowledge, had subconsciously accumulated a large amount of information, all of it pertaining to the past, and then, again subconsciously, had dramatized the material into the long and detailed stories which she wrote.

But if this was true, what was the source from which this vast amount of knowledge came to Mrs. Curran? Many of the details that came through the Ouija board to her were known to only a few historians. Assuming that a process of mental dissociation, followed by a dramatization of unconscious material, did actually occur to Mrs. Curran, how did her subconscious mind organize the material into novels, plays and poetry? These questions have never yet been successfully answered.

The Ouija board is one of several methods of reaching and communicating with an individual's subconscious mind. Some parapsychologists believe that the individual section of the subconscious is only a small portion of a huge subconscious region. These specialists state that, in this region below the personal subconscious, it may be possible to tune in to other stages of reality which are nevertheless completely unknown to our conscious selves.

You may ask—why experiment with the Ouija board? Well, I personally am intensely curious and the idea that I can get messages from my inner self is very appealing to me. Some of these messages will be coming from the first level of my personal subconscious, which in everyone is often highly unreliable but nevertheless most interesting. After considerable practice, you will usually find that you are able to recognize from which level of the subconscious the information is coming. Just as archaeologists study the Earth's physical layers to determine the nature of civilizations long past, so should the psychologist study the layers of the human subconscious because knowledge of these reveals man's mental and psychic history.

It should be pointed out that, although infrequent, there may be hazards in trying to make contact with your inner self. Psychologists caution that no one who has even the slightest mental or emotional instability should experiment with *automatism*, which is the lack of conscious control. Anyone who undertakes this kind of psychic experimentation must have sufficient intellectual competence and maturity to evaluate properly the material that will be coming through.

I once read of a case that nearly had a tragic ending. Two high school girls started to operate a Ouija board. It happened that both of these girls had lost their fathers through death. At first, everything went fine; one of the girls appeared to contact her dead father. The spirit who spoke to her through the Ouija board seemed to know all about her, giving detailed evidence which seemed to prove this. Then a spirit claiming to be a friend of her father's came through; this spirit also claimed to have been her "spirit guide" for many years.

This apparently reliable evidence served to "hook" the girl's belief. Presently the message came, "Life doesn't hold much for you, dear. It's such a beautiful world over here, you had better come over and join us." The girl slashed her wrists with a razor blade but mercifully survived. The other girl received almost the same advice from her "father." However, she received it with suspicion, refusing to act upon it.

Parapsychologists would give two possible explanations for the events in this case. Both girls were fatherless. They obviously needed father figures, and quite possibly they found life difficult without a father's support. Thus, the para-psychologists might say it is possible that from each girl's subconscious mind the "death wish"—which is inherent within all of us—came to the surface in the form of a piece of "good advice" from an apparently loving father.

The second explanation is that if what came to the girls through the Ouija board was indeed a genuine spirit communication, then the spirit communicating was certainly not the father, in either case, but rather some low-grade, malicious entity which was controlling the writing, masquerading as the father, getting information from the girls' own memories of the father, and trying to wreck their lives. Often, the personalities of young people who experiment with automatism are still in a formative and therefore unstable period; such experimentation is therefore dangerous for them.

Assuming that what emerges from experimentation with the Ouija board is only of subconscious origin, it would be advisable for all experimenters to have at least some elementary knowledge of what "depth psychology" is about. A book like Sigmund Freud's *Psychopathology of Everyday Life*, which is very easy to read, will alert most people to some of the tricks which our subconscious minds can play on us in order to circumvent the censorship imposed on anti-social behavior or emotional attitudes disapproved of by our conscious minds.

17

Keep One Foot on the Ground

My good friend, Dan Mather, became interested in psychic phenomena at about the same time I did. Unfortunately, he did not "keep one foot on the ground," and he suffered a disastrous consequence. Scientific researchers in this field warn all laymen to cease investigating if they are even slightly unstable emotionally. It is imperative that you do "keep one foot on the ground"—meaning, don't spend all your spare time perusing psychic matters.

Friend Dan, who was in the automobile business, often had much spare time to spend as he pleased. And it pleased him to spend every extra moment experimenting in the field of psychic phenomena—Ouija board, automatic writing, the pendulum, seances, astral-projection, and hallucinogenic drugs.

Dan really didn't have a chance because there were three strikes against him, and it would have taken only one strike to count him out in this particular game. He was just a little emotionally unstable. Nevertheless, he experimented day and night, unceasingly. Toward the end, he even took LSD. I begged him to back off, but he wouldn't listen.

"Dick," he said, "I have joined a group of professional men who meet once a week. Among them are doctors, attorneys, a college professor, even a well-known politician. Our LSD experience is truthfully a voyage into paradise. I have asked them if you could join us, and they are all affirmative. Words cannot describe the beauty and joy of this experience, and I'm delighted that you're going to share this adventure with us."

"Hold on there, Danny," I said. "This is an adventure I'm not sharing with you. No, no, the drug scene is not for me."

"But this is different, Dick."

"No, it's not, Danny," I said. "I tell you you're heading for big trouble if you continue this pattern. And listen, old buddy, you're spending far too much time on your occult interests. Haven't you been neglecting Gina and the boys?"

"Well, I guess she and the boys aren't too happy with me, but, Dick, this is such an important experience!"

Neither of us gave an inch. A couple of weeks later, he telephoned and said, a little sheepishly, "One of our famous modern-day prophets announced that the earth was going to shift on its poles, causing the entire United States to be inundated. He said the only safe place would be in Vancouver, British Columbia. Since this was supposed to happen last Sunday, I put Gina and the boys in the car and we drove up to Vancouver. Wow, are they mad at me! I guess I did go off half-cocked."

Intrinsically, my friend Danny was no dummy. He had a degree in business administration from Oregon State University. My degree is in English Literature, and I can recall Danny's telling me, one time, "I couldn't stand English and I almost flunked the required course in English Comp, my first year in college."

So you can imagine my shock at what I am going to report next. This happened shortly before Danny's incarceration in the State of Oregon Mental Hospital.

Dan said to me one day, "Dick, the most remarkable thing is happening to me. I can hear voices in my head. I ask them questions and they answer me."

"Danny," I sadly replied, "you're just about over the hill. I'm seriously concerned about you. You need help, old friend. Won't you let me make an appointment for you with a doctor?"

"No, no, I'm fine, Dick. It's just these voices that I can hear in my head. Here, let me show you. You ask me a question, then I'll ask them, and you'll see."

Okay, I thought. There is one field that Danny doesn't like. He has always avoided it so strenuously that it's doubtful whether even his subconscious has any knowledge of English Literature.

So I said, "All right, Danny, ask them to discuss the main tenets of Dryden and Pope, and their influence on eighteenth-century literature." Dan's eyes rolled back in their sockets, and his body stiffened for a moment. Then from his mouth began to pour an astoundingly erudite dissertation on Dryden and Pope.

"Wait! Not so fast!" I cried. "Wait until I find some paper, to take some of this down."

He stopped talking. I looked at him. His face was drained of color. His eyes looked more normal now but they seemed glazed.

I got some paper. "All right now, Danny, start again." He did, and I took notes. The contents of what he said could have come only from a scholar who had spent a lifetime researching the works and the lives of Dryden and Pope. I was unfamiliar with much of the material, although I recalled some of it from a college course I had taken in eighteenth-century literature, many years before.

Because it was difficult to believe that all this material that Dan had poured forth could be accurate, I later spent several hours at the library, checking it out. It checked out one hundred percent correct though none of this voluminous material could possibly have been in Dan's subconscious. Then where had it come from? Could an alien consciousness have taken over Dan's mind and vocal cords? I'm not sure, but it is possible.

Psychiatrists would explain what happened, by saying that Dan, at this point, had become paranoid, and that dementia praecox, or a split personality, had developed. In other words, psychiatrists would say that Dan was mentally ill; that another personality within his own subconscious had come through, and it was this other personality which had given the remarkable discourse on Dryden and Pope.

I imagined myself speaking to a psychiatrist. "But, Doctor, where did this personality get the information?"

The Doctor answers, "At some time in Dan's life, he was exposed to this material, and it was recorded in his subconscious mind."

Maybe. Yet it was very, very doubtful, because I know Dan. He simply would not have allowed himself to be exposed to this material. Therefore, how could this vast amount of information have been lodged in his subconscious at all? However, I will agree, in part, with the psychiatrist. Something unfortunate was certainly happening to Dan, and he needed help.

I appealed to him at least to stop taking LSD. But, no, I couldn't convince him. He was on a beautiful, exciting trip which was leading him directly into the arms of the Creator. Speaking of trips, he casually mentioned that he was experimenting with astral projection*; but didn't want to

---

*Astral projection or OOBE (out-of-body experience): The astral, or secondary body, removes itself from the physical body in sleep, trance, or during serious illness, and travels outside the periphery of the flesh. This excursion may be either conscious or unconscious. There will be more about this later.

discuss it until he had become more proficient in his astral travels.

"Please, Danny, be very careful," I warned. "You know how dangerous astral travel can be."

"Yes, yes, I know," he replied.

Wondering if I could throw a scare into him, I said, "You know, Danny, years before bodies were embalmed after death, the deceased would occasionally be disinterred for various reasons—such as the family wanting the body to be buried in another location, or the body being exhumed because of suspicion of foul play, and so forth. Well, Danny, it was often discovered that the supposed deceased person had come back to life after interment, and had desperately tried to get out of the casket. Some of the fingernails had been torn off and there were markes on the interior of the casket, proving that desperate attempts had been made to escape.

"Of course," I said, "in this country, where embalming is generally practiced nowadays, it is doubtful that this could occur. Nevertheless, as you know, often when astral projection has taken place, your body is more than semi-comatose. If a doctor checked your pulse, your respiration, and your eyes for dilation at that time, he would pronounce you dead.

"Now, what if you had difficulty getting back into your material body? We know this can happen, and it does. Would you wake up in a prep room on a table, just as the embalmer was about to aspirate you? Some reputable parapsychologists believe that, years ago, and even today, many people who have been pronounced medically dead are not dead, but are merely on an astral voyage. This is a chilling thought, Danny, but it could happen to you. I want you to think it over."

I hoped I might be getting to him now. He was frowning, and he seemed somewhat disturbed.

Then with a shrug he said, "Yeah, I know, Dick. I know I have to be careful, but I know how to protect myself. And say, listen, tonight our LSD group meets, and we're going to try a little mescaline this time. Why don't you come with me? Come on! It'll be great! You've already been invited, you know."

"No way, Danny. Thanks just the same. I know you want to share what you think is going to be a glorious experience, and I appreciate your intentions, old friend. But you're on the wrong track, Danny, and I'm terribly concerned about you. Please, please knock off this drug kick you're on, and—"

He interrupted. "Don't you worry about me. I've got everything under control." Just two days after this, his wife and his mother had him committed to the State Mental Hospital. Mutual friends called and gave me the bad news.

They also told me a very strange story which I later verified with Gina, Danny's wife. It happened on Danny's last night at home, before his incarceration.

Dan, his wife, and their two sons were seated at the dinner table. Dan had eaten nothing, nor had he said a word during the entire meal. Suddenly, a strange expression came over his face, his eyes glazed, his head fell forward, and he started to snore softly.

Gina sighed and said, "Boys, I think you know your Dad has been sick for some time. Your grandmother and I have been talking, and we feel he should go to a hospital for treatment."

The phone rang. One of the boys ran to answer it. "It's for you, Mom," he said.

Gina picked up the receiver. It was a friend calling. "Say, Gina, will you come right over here and get Danny? He's out on our front porch, and he has his nose pressed against the dining-room window. He has an awfully peculiar look on his face, Gina, and his eyes seem to be rolled back in his head. He looks as if he's asleep. He seems to be snoring. Tom is out of town tonight and the girls and I had just sat down to eat. Frankly we're frightened."

"Oh, Ann," said Gina, "you're mistaken. Dan is sitting right here at the dinner table. I'll admit he's not his usual self. For one thing, he's asleep, with his eyes open, but all you can see are the whites of his eyes. Oh, there! Now he's awake and smiling, and—"

"Gina, he's gone," said Ann. "I was watching him while you were talking. When you said, 'Oh, there, now he's awake,' he just simply vanished! Hang on a minute. I'll look out on the porch."

In a calm voice, Dan, at the dinner table, said, "I've just had a pleasant dream. I saw Ann and the girls—Tom wasn't there—sitting at their dining-room table for dinner. They were having a tuna fish casserole and an avocado salad."

Ann came back and picked up the phone. "There is no one out on the porch now, Gina, but there's a mark on the window where Dan's nose was pressing."

"What are you having for dinner tonight, Ann?" It was a tuna fish casserole and an avocado salad.

Late that night, Gina and the boys were awakened by screams, and they heard the front door crash open. Jumping out of bed, they dashed to a front window. They were just in time to see Dan, in his pajamas, running at full speed down the street, shrieking at the top of his lungs. Gina flew to the telephone. It was time to make the dreaded call.

A few weeks later, I received a letter from Dan. He was now a patient in the Oregon State Mental Hospital. The letter was pathetic, but it was rational.

As soon as he arrived at the hospital, he wrote that he had been placed in a ward with the criminally insane. The letter went on:

> I knew I was not normal but I most certainly did not belong with the criminally insane. It was a horrible and frightening experience. I'm convinced my problem is a case of spirit possession. There are times when I can feel this personality take over my body. Usually, I black out, and when I regain consciousness, I have no memory of what has happened. I know what you're thinking, Dick, and you're wrong. It's not my own secondary personality that is taking over, although I wish this were the case.
>
> You were right about one thing. I didn't keep one foot on the ground and I probably shouldn't have experimented with mind-altering drugs. It appears that due to bad judgment, I opened myself up for possession and, therefore, I have some unpleasant days ahead. Today, one of the doctors informed me that I am scheduled for a series of electric shock treatments. If the results are favorable, I'll be able to return home in a couple of months. Incidentally, one of the nurses agrees with my possession diagnosis. She thinks the shock treatments will be as effective as an exorcism rite. We shall see.

A few months later, Dan came home, apparently cured. At our first meeting, he said, "I was permitted to read only part of my hospital report. It said schizophrenia and dementia praecox. Treatment was electric shock therapy, and it was successful. Perhaps I did have those mental disorders, but in addition I'm absolutely positive that an undesirable alien personality somehow or other took took over my body."

Today, Dan is leading a peaceful, normal life. He is still interested in psychic phenomena, reading every new book that comes out on the subject. Does he still occasionally experiment?

"No sir," he says. "I'm like an alcoholic who has been in a sanitarium for treatment. He doesn't dare take that first drink. Sure, I had a solid glimpse of heaven when I was taking those hallucinogenic drugs, and it was glorious. But other things happened that were just the opposite of glorious, and if there is a hell, I was there, too. I know now, in my particular case, I should have kept both feet on the ground."

18

Phenomena in Fiji

For many years, our business took us to the South Pacific via cruise ship. In Suva, Fiji, we were fortunate to meet Dr. and Mrs. Harry Pennington. For six months of the year, the Penningtons lived on a beautiful estate a few miles from Suva. The other six months, they resided in Laguna Beach, California. The hospitable Penningtons insisted that we spend an afternoon with them at their home, snorkle diving, followed by an authentic Fijian dinner prepared by their own native cook.

A multitude of colorful tropical fish that would gently nibble on our toes were a delight. So was the hyperpalatable native dinner we devoured. Most interesting of all were the stories about psychic phenomena on the Fijian Islands, that Dr. Pennington related to me. But, first, who was Dr. Pennington?

Fifteen years previously, the U.S. Health Department had sent Dr. Pennington, with a staff of eighteen medical research doctors, to the Fijian Islands. The mission had a twofold purpose. First, Dr. Pennington was to attempt to develop a cure for leprosy. He didn't find a cure but he did develop a serum that would arrest this dreadful disease; as a result, he was a runner-up for the Nobel Prize in Medicine that year.

The second purpose of his assignment was to discover why the birthrate was falling so alarmingly in the Fijian Islands; and in a short time he did have the answer to this problem.

Dr. Pennington found that the native Fijian drink, Kava, is a narcotic. To me, Kava tastes like bitter, muddy water. It is derived from the Kava root. The doctor found that Kava, if taken in excess, will kill most of the sperm in the male semen. Tests showed that the native men had been increasing their Kava intake for the past few years. As a result, their sperm count had dropped greatly.

Pennington said it was most amusing to hear the reasons the native men gave, for not wanting to reduce their Kava intake. Most of them declared that the pressures and tensions of civilized living were so intense that they needed more Kava to relax them. Actually, the life-style of the native Fijian men had not changed in fifty years; to them, pressures and tensions are nearly nonexistent.

"Indeed," said Dr. Pennington, "fifty years ago some tribes were still practicing cannibalism. Their pressures should have been greater then—no one knew who was going to eat whom next."

When I asked him if he had had any psychic experiences in the Islands, his eyes lit up. He said, "I certainly did. I'll tell you some true stores and save the best for the last.

"A few years ago, I was treating some natives who were building a road and bridges on an island nearby. They had unexpectedly run out of material and needed several barrels of nails, some special lengths of lumber, plus a number of other items. I asked the native foreman how he was going to order the material—he had no phone, and the town was over fifty miles away. He smiled and tapped his head.

" 'It will be here in two hours and a half,' he said. 'You will see.' A material order through thought transference? Ridiculous!

The foreman then closed his eyes and silently moved his lips. Opening his eyes, he said, 'The order is now being filled. You will see.'

"I most certainly did see," continued Dr. Pennington, smiling, "because exactly two and a half hours later an old truck came chugging up the road. In it were all the items the foreman had ordered! As a scientist, I found it very difficult to accept this phenomenon.

"Here's another incident you might enjoy. A friend of ours is the business manager of the Suva Hospital. She is a widow, and she had been telling us about her ninety-year-old mother, who is blind. Her mother lives alone in an upstairs room above a drugstore, and she apparently has occult powers. I thought the stories our friend had been telling us, about things her mother could do, were ridiculous, yet our friend was so rational in all other areas that I finally decided I had better investigate this allegedly gifted old lady. Our friend seemed very pleased that I wished to visit her mother.

"When we arrived at the foot of the stairs leading to the old lady's room, our friend clasped my arm and said, 'If we go up the stairs very quietly, when you get to the top you can look through a window that's in the door, and you will see my mother in a rocking chair. You will see something else, too, and it will baffle you.'

"Furtively we climbed the stairs. When we reached the top I looked through the window. Sure enough, there was the old native lady wrapped in a black shawl, rocking away in her chair. I could see that her mouth was moving, as if she were talking, and her face was turned toward another rocking chair that was right next to hers. This chair was unoccupied, but it was also rocking.

" 'Whom is she talking to, and what is causing that chair to rock?' I asked my friend.

" 'She is talking to an old friend who died many years ago. Of course, you and I can't see this friend but I really believe Mother does. As for the chair rocking, I guess her friend is rocking it. Would you like to meet Mother now?'

"When we entered the room, the rocking ceased in both chairs, and the little old lady, her wrinkled face creased in a gentle toothless smile, slowly rose to her feet. 'I knew you were coming today, Doctor,' she said. 'My daughter has told me so many wonderful things about you and your wife.'

"After a few moments' exchange of pleasantries, I asked, 'How do you make this chair rock?'

"She cocked her head, as if she were listening to something, then replied, 'My friend rocks in this chair, sir.' Now the chair began rocking again. 'My friend says you have done much good for the Fijian people, and she joins me in offering you deep thanks.'

"There was certainly no one else in that room, but the unoccupied chair was rocking merrily away.

"I pointed to the chair," said Dr. Pennington, "and asked, 'May I sit in that chair?'

" 'You will be sitting on my friend's lap,' the old lady replied, 'but she won't mind.'

"Well, I sat down in the chair. I could feel no one's lap under me, yet the chair continued to rock and I could not make it stop. I planted my feet hard on the floor and stiffened my body and my legs. It made no difference whatever. The chair kept on rocking.

"My legs, arms and back were beginning to hurt, so I stood up. The chair stopped rocking. Both ladies were smiling at me. The daughter could see what must have been a shocked expression on my face. The mother couldn't see, but she had certainly been able to hear my grunts and snorts as I tried vainly to prevent the chair from rocking.

"Then the old lady said to me, 'Now you watch me go down the stairs. You will have big surprise.'

"This was certainly the understatement of the century! What I saw next led me to wonder whether I had completely lost contact with reality. That old lady put one hand on the banister, then slowly and steadily walked down those stairs. But good Lord! Her feet were not touching the stairs! They were at least four inches above the stair treads!

"Twice I yelled, 'Stop!' And she stopped. I felt her arm. No tension in it. I lifted her frail hand from the banister, then placed it back on the railing. No tension. I realized that my hunch had been wrong. Anyway, how could a ninety-year-old woman support the weight of her whole body on one hand? It was doubtful if even a gymnast could accomplish this.

"I put my hand between her feet and the stair tread. There was nothing under her feet. I had thought there might be a mirror. But no, she was simply suspended in air. Or perhaps, to put it more accurately, I was witnessing actual levitation. Of course, this was scientifically impossible.

"Well," continued Dr. Pennington, "I thought of one more thing to try. I put both my hands under her shoes and I lifted—with all my strength. Her body raised slightly, but oh, it was so heavy! I estimated about 175 pounds, yet this little old lady could not have weighed an ounce over 85 pounds.

"I lifted again, straining. This time her body raised only a fraction, and I heard her murmur, 'Be careful, young man, you might hurt yourself.'

"She was right. Furthermore, I could see that I was getting nowhere. I thanked the two ladies for the interesting experience they had given me, excused myself, and went back to my lab—where I accomplished absolutely nothing for the rest of the day.

"That night when I told my wife about the experience, she laughed and said, 'Why, Harry, haven't you talked to any of the natives about the supernatural? Just wait until you get into voodoo.' A few weeks later I did happen to witness an incident of voodoo that further disturbed my equanimity.

"This is the way it happened," said Dr. Pennington. "My work took me to the lovely island of Rora Tonga, where I was to stay for three weeks. One day, the houseboy of the associate with whom I was staying told us that he was going to kill an enemy whom he had not seen or been in contact with for over six months. The enemy lived with his family in a village about forty miles away. The houseboy said that the moment he stuck a pin into the chest of a doll resembling his enemy, the enemy himself would fall to the ground, dead.

"My associate, who had spent several years on Rora Tonga, told me that he himself had witnessed several deaths by voodoo. The power of death by suggestion in these cases had been ruled out, because the victims, in the deaths he had witnessed, did not know they were scheduled for execution.

"Before I could believe any of this nonsense, I said I would have to see it myself. So I arranged a test. On the day the houseboy was going to kill his enemy, my associate would arrange to be with him. My associate would witness the pinsticking voodoo ceremony, and the moment the pin entered the doll's chest, he would write down the time.

"Meanwhile, I arranged my own schedule so that I would be in the victim's house that day—forty miles away—to give the entire family inoculations which they sorely needed. Then if anything happened—and I doubted it would—I would record the time.

"I drove to the enemy's village and easily found the house of the intended victim. The father and mother and eight children lived in a small hut with a thatched roof. Because the three youngest children were in poor health, I promised to return soon and treat them; also to give everyone their booster shots.

"The next day, the houseboy announced that he would kill his enemy in a few hours. I jumped into the jeep and drove rapidly to the village. When I got there, the father was very much alive—which was no surprise to me. I started the inoculations with the kids, at the same time watching the father out of the corner of my eye.

"I had inoculated about half of the children, when all at once I saw the father clutch his chest, then fall flat on his face. My heart beat faster. It had really happened! But it occurred to me that this must be simply a remarkable coincidence. Very likely, I said to myself, the sight of the needle had caused this man to faint. I had seen that kind of reaction many times before. Nevertheless, I checked my watch and wrote down the time.

"Then I rolled the man over on his back and—oh-oh—he certainly didn't look good. He was not good. He was dead. Later, with the widow's permission, I did an autopsy, but could find no cause for death. The man's heart was perfect.

"Yes," said Dr. Pennington, "you guessed it. My associate and I compared slips of paper. He had written down: 'Pin entered doll chest at 2:08:30 p.m.' I had written down: 'Man lost consciousness and fell to floor at 2:08:30 p.m.'

"And now, Richard," Dr. Pennington finished, "comes my final dissertation. I told you I was leaving the best for last, and I believe you will find this adventure most intriguing.

"An invitation to a seance, to be held on a nearby island, was presented to me. I was informed that I was the first white man ever to be invited to attend such a function there. Because my scientific skepticism had been severely shaken by my two previous encounters with the paranormal, I was eager to expand my knowledge in this non-material area. In the event that something unusual might happen during this seance, I meant to go prepared.

"I replenished the supplies in my medical bag, adding one small item—a sterilized pin. If phenomena should occur, I intended to prick myself with this pin. If I felt any pain, it would prove that I was not hallucinating, nor hypnotized. This was just a little safeguard, although I didn't really believe I would need to use the pin." Dr. Pennington smiled as he remembered.

"Well," he said, "I entered a large hut with the usual dirt floor. In attendance I found about a dozen adult natives. I had noticed several children playing outside the hut as I came in. After formal introductions, a communal bowl of Kava was passed around the group; I urged the men to be extremely temperate. 'If you take more than one sip,' I warned them, 'your women will bear no children, and the Fijian people will vanish from the earth.' However, they were not impressed. To my one small sip they took several large gulps.

"Then one of the men called a small naked boy, about ten years old, into the hut, from the children playing outside. Glowering, the man pointed a finger at the child and in Fijian said, 'Do it now.'

"The boy immediately fell to the floor in convulsions. Instinctively I moved forward to help the child, but two of the men restrained me. 'He will be all right,' one said. 'You watch now.'

"I watched and what I saw was so astounding that I almost forgot about my sterilized pin. The boy stiffened, appearing to go into a catatonic trance. What happened next simply defies logical explanation.

From all of that child's orifices a vaporous, foggy-like substance emitted. Right there in front of my eyes, this sub-stance formed into a huge Fijian man. By this time I had taken the pin out of my bag and was furiously pricking my leg. I felt every prick—which ruled out hallucination. I was mildly suspicious that perhaps a hallucinogenic drug had been placed in the bowl of Kava, yet the one small sip I had taken certainly would not produce such an apparition as this!

"In a booming voice, the materialized native told me that he lived six hundred years ago. He had been a prince, he said. I sat there interrogating him for about half an hour, and—having considerable knowledge of Fijian history and culture—I tried to trap him. However, every question I asked, he answered completely and accurately.

"Then I asked him if in the interest of medical science I could examine him physically. He replied favorably, but said I would have to hurry because his time was limited in this dimension. Nearly everything checked out perfectly—blood pressure, respiration, heart, response to pain. There was just one thing about which I was suspicious, and that was his superficial fascia, his skin. To me, his skin did not appear normal. Both color and substance were not quite right. I wanted very much to take a wedge—a biopsy—but felt I ought not to inflict any further pain on this giant. Further-more, he was becoming restless.

"Abruptly, he said he must now leave; he had duties to perform in his state of vibrations. Then his body distorted; it rapidly turned into a shapeless mass of gray vapor, which flowed back into the orifices of the boy lying there on the dirt floor. Again, I stuck the pin into my leg, repeatedly; I still felt the pain. But this entire experience was so mind-boggling that I almost wished I had not felt the pin enter my flesh, thereby giving me an explanation, vapid as it might have been.

"I examined the child," went on Dr. Pennington, "and I could detect no sign of life whatever. He was not breathing, and the pupils of his eyes were dilated. Fearing he had actually expired, I started mouth-to-mouth resuscitation. At that point, two of the natives jerked me roughly to my feet and said, 'Do not touch him again. He will be all right.'

"Sure enough, in just another moment the child's eyes flickered, then opened, and with a smile he jumped up to his feet and ran back out of the hut, to join the other children at play. It was obvious that he had been totally unaware of all that had occurred in the past hour.

"I have related this experience to several of my colleagues," said Dr. Pennington, "and most of their reactions were similar. 'Come, come, Harry, do you expect me to believe this tripe?' Or, 'Now, Harry, you've been drinking too much Kava.' Or, 'Pin or no pin, you were certainly hallucinating.' Or, 'Why, Harry, I'm surprised at you! And to think you are the man who almost won the Nobel prize in Medicine last year!' "

Dr. Pennington smiled. "Well, Dick," he said, "what would you have replied, in rebuttal to these scoffing, learned associates of mine? I'll tell you what I said, 'All right, gentlemen, do you think you possess strong intelligences? If you do, you must have open minds, even though you may be healthfully skeptical at the same time. Well, it appears to me that you have forgotten what you have been taught about a singular facet of human behavior—that is, the tendency to reject the strange and unexpected, even when evidence confronts your own eyes.

" 'I'll give you an example of this,' I told them. 'Recently two professors at an eastern university performed an experiment. They dressed up several students as apparitions and arranged for them to be on the campus in the middle of the night. They plotted the routes of these students so they would meet several professors, who would at that time be crossing the campus after a late meeting.

" 'And now take notice of this. Those luminous white figures met those professors at eight different times, yet not one professor reported having observed any unusual occurrence! The dressed-up students reported that they had seen no surprised looks and heard no astonished exclamations. Of course, it's possible,' I said, 'that if any of the professors actually did take conscious note of the apparitions, they may have felt reluctant to expose themselves to ridicule by reporting it. Or perhaps they simply rejected mentally the sight of what they met, since this was an inordinate departure from what is generally accepted as normal.

" 'Remember this, gentlemen, man is subject to over 10,000 impressions every second, on every level of his responsiveness. If he had to be consciously aware of each of these impressions, he would be totally disoriented and unable to function. Thus, we learn to single out, and respond to, only those impressions which fit the accepted version of reality which we have learned. Whenever a deviation occurs, and if the deviation is not too extreme, we will account for it within this accepted version, which is for us the norm. When a completely alien deviation comes along, it threatens our very sanity, so we reject it. Any changes, even small ones, in what we accept as reality have to be introduced gradually, if they are to fit into this accepted reality.

" 'Well, gentlemen,' I told them," said Dr. Pennington, smiling broadly, " 'the phenomenon which I personally witnessed, and which I have just described to you, violates all that is accepted in our current version of reality. Therefore you are inclined to ridicule it at once, without giving it even a cursory examination. Then you turn your backs and mutter that it's obviously an illusion. This is because you can't define it as verifiable reality, with your current concepts of science. What I experienced was no illusion, I assure you, and I was not hallucinating.

" 'I myself,' I told them, 'wanted at first to excuse my own skepticism by saying that the human personality has definite limitations. Then, somewhere deep inside me, a voice commanded me to believe that the human personality has *no* limitations except those which it accepts, and that the impossible, and the highly unlikely, because of an amazingly explosive technology, have already moved into the realm of the possible. And that, gentlemen,' I said to them, 'is where I stand in this matter. I rest my case.' "

Dr. Pennington laughed and added, "Nobody said anything at first. Then one of the men, who had been unequivocally critical and singularly vituperative, said in a very small voice, 'Harry, do you have a couple of aspirin?' "

19

Unorthodox Healing

My good friend Chinky was terminally ill with multiple myeloma (the imposing name given to cancer of the bone marrow). Chinky telephoned me one day and asked if I would drive him out in the country to a farmhouse where, he had heard, many remarkable healings had taken place.

A friend had told Chinky about this farmer, a Mr. Johnson, who apparently had some sort of healing electricity in his hands when he placed them over the affected part of the body. You didn't have to tell him the location of your ailment, said Chinky's friend. Mr. Johnson would pass his hands over your body, and tell you!

We finally found the farm, though not without some difficulty, and I helped Chinky walk into a large, screened porch, which apparently was Mr. Johnson's reception room. More than a dozen people were sitting there—most of them, by their appearance, as terminally ill as my friend. A heavy-set woman came to meet us, introducing herself as Mrs. Johnson. She wrote our names on a piece of paper, then held out to us an empty coffee can. She instructed us to deposit in it $2 for the treatment which her husband would administer. She hastened to explain that this was an offering or donation. The law, she said, forbade their charging a fee for the treatment.

Chinky put in $4 and said we would both get a treatment. This was because on the drive out I had complained that my right kidney was aching; I fervently hoped a stone was not developing.

We sat there for about an hour. Then Mrs. Johnson called Chinky's name, and with her help he hobbled painfully into the house. About ten minutes later he reappeared, and I could scarcely believe what I saw! His face had regained its normal color. He was no longer bent over, he was walking alone, and he was not limping! Could this be the man who ten minutes ago had not been able to walk without help?

He sat down and said to me, "Dick! I've had the most amazing experience! Mrs. Johnson told me to lie down on the kitchen table in there. Then this man came into the kitchen. He passed his hands over my entire body, but he scarcely touched even my clothing! Then he said—just like that!— 'You are suffering from cancer of the bone marrow. I can't help you much unless you stop taking radiation treatments.'"

Chinky stared at me, wide-eyed. "How did he know what my disease is, Dick? And how did he know I'm taking radiation treatments for it? Well, anyway, he rolled me over gently onto my stomach and placed his hands lightly on my spine. I could feel a tremendous heat coming from his hands, and the pain in my body started to leave! He said I would feel fine for an hour, after which I would have a recurrence of the pain.

"What do you think, Dick?" asked Chinky, in all seriousness. "Shall I stop the X-ray therapy and come back to Mr. Johnson and get some treatments?"

Well, I told Chinky what I honestly thought. At that time I felt that medical science was his best chance, so I said, "No, Chinky, I think you had better continue the radiation therapy you are having. When that series is completed, then we'll come back to Mr. Johnson." (I have bitterly regretted telling Chinky that, because he did not live long enough to complete his course of X-ray treatments.)

Mrs. Johnson now told me that I was next. She led me into the kitchen and asked me to lie on the table. A tall man in overalls came in. His hands were enormous, and he had no fingernails. I was about to ask him how he lost his nails, when he placed those enormous hands over my lower abdomen. "You had an exploratory appendectomy several years ago, didn't you?" he asked. "Not a good closure, either."

Good Lord, I thought, could he see the scar through my clothing? But he was going right on. He placed his hands on my chest. "You have a sliding hiatal hernia," he said. "It bothers you when you are overweight, right?" He was certainly right!

Next he rolled me over on my stomach, barely touching my buttocks. "Oh-oh!" he said. "You have had a hemorrhoidectomy and the removal of a triple fistula . . . that wasn't much fun, was it?" How in the world could this man know these things? I was totally bewildered.

He then placed his hand over my right kidney. "Now I'm dissolving a stone that was forming," he said. "In a minute or two the pain will be gone." I felt much heat coming from his hand, which was somewhat heavy on my back, but motionless. And, by golly, it was hard to believe it, but the pain was leaving!

I gratefully asked, "How do you do this, Mr. Johnson? And how do you get your hands so warm? Do you put them in an oven?"

"Hold on, Mr. Walker," he laughed. "One question at a time! How do I heal? Apparently some kind of healing electricity or energy comes out of my hands. No, I don't put them in an oven. They automatically become very warm the second I put them near a person who needs healing. The pain in your kidney has gone, hasn't it?"

"It certainly has!" I replied.

"All right," he said. "Now take hold of my hands. Do they feel warm?"

"Not a bit," I said, "but they were downright hot a couple of minutes ago."

"The heat left them because you no longer needed healing," he told me. "The kidney stone which was forming has been dissolved, and your hiatal hernia is dormant at present. These two problems won't become acute again for a long time; maybe never. But to be on the safe side, you should come back for one more treatment.

"Now," he went on, "regarding your friend who has this terrible bone marrow cancer, I think I can cure him; but he will have to stop taking the X-ray treatments. The treatments are not compatible with the healing energy force that comes from my hands, even though I have temporarily stopped the destructive action of the cancer cells, and given him a short period of relief from pain."

"Well, Mr. Johnson," I said, "your skills are certainly most remarkable and effective. How are you able to tell what's wrong with a person who comes to you? You said I have a hiatal hernia, and you used other medical terms. Have you studied medicine, or worked in a hospital? And how can you diagnose so accurately?"

"Mr. Walker, I know nothing about medicine. During the depression I was going to high school, but I had to quit in my third year, to help my folks on the farm. About the way I diagnose—all I can tell you is that when I pass my hands over a person's body, the moment they are over an area that has been or is ailing, they automatically stop, and words come into my head. I don't know where the words come from, but they always seem to be right...at least that's what my patients tell me."

He caught himself, and smiled at me. "I guess I shouldn't be referring to any of these people as patients. If I did that, I'd get in trouble. A lawyer who has been coming here for some time for treatment told me I mustn't charge fees, because I'm not a licensed doctor. But I can accept donations. Well, Mr. Walker, I have to get back to work now, because I have a porch full of sick people waiting for me."

I held him another minute. "One last question, Mr. Johnson. Do you think you are healing people, or is God healing them through you?"

He shook his head. "I don't think God has anything to do with it. It seems pretty obvious that I'm the one who is doing the healing. And, frankly, it's an easy way to earn a living, compared to farm work. It makes me feel good, too, to be helping people who need me."

On the way home, Chinky's terrible pain returned. Mr. Johnson had told him it would. Chinky gritted his teeth and said to me, "When I'm through with these miserable X-ray treatments we'll come back and see Mr. Johnson again. I can't tell you how wonderful it's been, to be free from pain, if only for this short time." Only a week later, Chinky lost his battle. By that time he was confined to his bed at home, and even the very slightest movement of his body caused him agonizing pain.

The last time I saw Chinky, he said to me, "Dick, my doctor tells me I will die very soon. I'm not afraid to die, because I firmly believe that everyone has a spiritual body that survives death. If the whole mechanism of umbilical and 'silver' cord is true, then the process of death is exactly the same as the process of birth. In birth, the individual is not truly himself until he is first freed from the attachment to the matrix of the mother's womb, and in death, to the matrix of the physical body. When the labor pains of a human birth are prolonged or delayed, forcible action has to be taken to remove the baby, or to induce contractions."

Chinky nodded painfully at me. "I see by the expression on your face," he said, "that you have guessed what I'm leading up to. Yes, euthanasia. That's a Greek word, compounded from *eu* which means *good*, or *well*, and *thanatos*, meaning *death*. Euthanasia means good dying, dying well, dying without pain," said Chinky.

"And you know, Dick," he went on slowly, "primitive cultures were in many ways more civilized than our own. Behind their customs they had a whole reinforcement of religious beliefs, which made the customs possible and acceptable. I read of an interesting custom in seventeenth-century Brittany, where incurable patients had the right to ask for the Holy Stone. The relatives would gather, and the last rites would be given by the priest. Then the oldest relative would raise the Holy (and heavy) Stone in his hands, and let it fall on the patient's head."

Chinky stopped for a while, as if it were almost too much effort for him to talk. Presently he went on. "When the doctor was here today, I asked him to administer to me the equivalent of the Holy Stone. He said he could not do that. He said that would lose him his license to practice medicine, and I would just have to 'sweat it out' a little while longer. Well, Dick," said Chinky's dragging voice, "I have no perspiration left. So will you please call Mr. Johnson and have him come in and give me a treatment to relieve this pain? I'll donate any amount of money he wants. But get him here tonight. His number is on the pad by the phone downstairs."

I telephoned. Mrs. Johnson said her husband would be treating patients until midnight, and then he would have to get a few hours' sleep. They would come in at eight in the morning, and a $2 donation, plus gas, would be just fine.

At seven the next morning my phone rang. It was Chinky's wife, with a request. "Will you please call Mr. Johnson, Dick, and tell him not to come in. Early this morning, Chinky called me into his room. What he said was, 'I won't need the Holy Stone or Mr. Johnson. The pain has gone, and I'm going to let go now.' "

With those words my friend Chinky's terrible ordeal ended, and I thanked God that his fervent wish for euthanasia was fulfilled.

20

Spirit Doctors. . .Non-Infallible

A fascinating book by J. Bernard Hutton, entitled *Healing Hands*, tells of a former fireman who goes into trance, during which his body and brain are taken over by a deceased Dr. William Lang. Dr. Lang was one of England's most highly skilled ophthalmologists. The book is endorsed by The Royal British College of Medical Practitioners (an organization corresponding to our American Medical Association). It cites many case histories of remarkable cures, all of which have been thoroughly investigated and authenticated. Hutton, the author of the book, is a journalist.

The former fireman, Mr. George Chapman, had no medical training, and reliable investigators say there is no way his subconscious mind could have been exposed to surgical procedures and medical knowledge.

When Mr. Chapman removes a tumor, his hands do not touch the body of the patient. Qualified surgeons, having closely observed his operations, reported that his hands moved skillfully, and at lightning speed, about two inches above the patient's body. An incision then appeared on the body, but with no bleeding; and the tumor ejaculated from the incision. Then the incision closed spontaneously, and a small white scar was all that was left.

Among the observing doctors were several who had worked with Dr. Lang. These doctors were of course familiar with Dr. Lang's techniques. They swore, under oath, that from the mouth of Mr. Chapman came the familiar voice of Dr. Lang, high-pitched and nasal, barking commands to his assistants (these latter were invisible to the surgeons in attendance). The techniques, also, were unmistakably those of Dr. Lang.

The only differences the doctors could detect were the tremendous speed of Mr. Chapman's hands, and the fact that his hands never at any time touched the body of the patient.

So many terminally ill people came to Mr. Chapman for treatment that he was forced to build a large clinic, and train several other men to go into trance and perform the same type of successful non-touching surgery. Bizarre as it seems, the clinic is allowed to operate with the full sanction of The Royal British College of Medical Practitioners. Furthermore, Mr. Chapman claims to send Spirit doctors all over the world, to effect cures while patients are asleep. Thus many desperately ill people, who cannot afford the trip to England, are able to receive treatment by writing to Mr. Chapman and requesting help.

Some years ago, a dear friend of ours, a man who developed a unique recreational program which received international acclaim, suffered a stroke which left him without speech and with an arm and a leg paralyzed. The usual therapy was unsuccessful in his case, and several years passed with no improvement. This vibrant personality, who had brought so much pleasure to people all over the world, was reduced to a dependent cripple without means of communication. It was a tragedy.

Then I happened to read the book *Healing Hands,* and I immediately thought, perhaps Fred can be helped after all! The address of Mr. Chapman's clinic in England was given in the book, for anyone who needed help. I wanted to write the clinic at once. First, of course, I asked Fred's wife for permission, and I gave her the book to read.

Having read it, she was as eager as I was, and she asked me to write to Mr. Chapman. There was nothing to lose. I wrote and Mr. Chapman replied promptly. In his letter he told me that Fred should be asleep when the Spirit doctors arrived. The time difference between London, England, and Portland, Oregon, was determined, and Mr. Chapman notified me that the examination and treatment would occur on the night of July 9.

This was only three night away. Fred's wife and I decided not to tell Fred about his forthcoming nocturnal treatment. He would be disappointed if nothing effective occurred. Furthermore, we really didn't have much faith in Spirit doctors.

Early on the morning of July 10, Fred's wife telephoned me in great excitement. "It just doesn't seem possible," she said, "but something must have happened to Fred during the night! A few minutes ago he clearly said, 'I want a toothbrush.'" This was indeed exciting because since Fred had been ill he had lost interest in personal grooming.

"These are the first words I've heard him speak in four years!" his wife said. "Then he walked toward the bathroom without using his crutch; he was actually swinging both arms and grinning happily at me! He did fall before he got into the bathroom," she said, "but he wasn't hurt and he refused to let me help him up. He's in the bathroom now," she said. "The door is open, so listen, maybe you can hear him humming."

I listened eagerly. Yes, I could faintly hear Fred humming "Thank Heaven for Little Girls." It was one of his favorite songs.

What were the odds that this was a coincidence? A trillion to one? Mr. Chapman had written me that the Spirit doctors would be treating Fred in his sleep on the night of July 9. Here on the morning of July 10 his wife was reporting a dramatic improvement in his condition. It was a gloriously happy day for me. I felt that I had had a share in starting Fred's incredibly sudden convalescence.

But that evening my elation changed to concern. Fred's wife telephoned again. She told me that Fred seemed to be continuing to improve, but that he had developed a severe case of hiccups. Though she had tried several remedies to help him, the hiccups had not stopped. So, now she was going to call the doctor.

The next day I learned that Fred was in the hospital. The doctors had been unable to stop his hiccuping. The prognosis was not good.

My concern turned to alarm. Had something gone wrong with the Spirit doctors' treatment? It would seem so. Two days later, Fred's daughter telephoned to inform us that her father had had a massive stroke, and was no longer with us.

My self-recriminations were bitter; it was my fault that Fred had died. Why couldn't I have minded my own business? But what had gone wrong? Had the Spirit doctors attempted to dissolve a clot, and in the process had they moved it to a location that had caused my friend's death?

Whatever the reason, I was nearly overcome with grief and guilt. The widow and her children said that they did not in any way blame me, but I feared that their true feelings coincided with mine. I wrote to Mr. Chapman and told him of my friend's sudden death. I asked him what went wrong.

He promptly replied, "I'm sorry we were unable to help your friend. The Spirit doctors' treatments are not always successful. Please believe me, Mr. Walker, your friend is much happier now than he was a short time ago."

21

Ouija-Board Enigma

Just how the Ouija board works has perplexed psychic researchers for many years. Today, scientists still do not have the answer, even though it seems to be an accepted fact that an involuntary muscular action is responsible for the movement of the planchette.

I will now consider several personal experiences with the Ouija board, which were indeed bewildering at the time, and which even now seem to defy logical explanation.

It seems indisputable that some people are more psychically sensitive than others. By the same token, they get quicker and better results when their fingertips are resting on the planchette. My wife's mother, Frances, was one of these psychic-sensitive persons, and so was her aunt, Louise Drexel. Louise and Frances had accompanied me to my second seance. Louise's husband, Mr. Frank Drexel—Uncle Frank—had passed away a few months before the event I am now going to describe.

Frances was living with us at that time, and one night she and I decided to play the Ouija board. As soon as we placed our fingertips on the planchette, it spelled out the name *Frank.*

I asked, "Is it you, Uncle Frank?"
The planchette darted to *yes.*
"Do you have a message for us?" I asked.
Yes.
"Is it for anyone in particular?"
Yes. Then it spelled out *Lou.*
"What do you want to tell Lou?" I asked.
Money it spelled.
"Where is the money?"
In pants.
"What pants?"
Gray Linen.
"In a pocket?" I asked.
Yes. Left back pocket, it spelled.
"Where are the pants?"
In wardrobe.
"Where is the wardrobe?" I asked.

Hanging on door of bedroom closet, it spelled. Then it spelled, *Call Lou, give her my love, and tell her I'm chipper.* When Uncle Frank was feeling especially good, he would say he was chipper.

This was interesting, but since both Frances and I knew that Uncle Frank used this word, it could possibly have come from our subconscious. Certainly, though, neither of us knew anything about money or pants in a wardrobe, so there was no possibility of a subconscious manifestation from us regarding these items.

I called Lou, who at that time was still living in her huge house on the Columbia River, at least 25 miles from us. I explained that her sister and I had been operating the Ouija board and Uncle Frank had sent her his love and was chipper. Then I asked, "Do you know of any gray linen pants of Uncle Frank's that might be in a wardrobe in the bedroom closet?"

"I don't think so," she replied. "Well, now, wait a minute. Frank had his wardrobe all packed for a trip we were going to take to Palm Springs, just before he became ill. I think the wardrobe is still hanging on the closet door. I've been sleeping in another room since he died."

"Okay, Auntie Lou," I said. "Will you please look in his wardrobe and see if there's a pair of gray linen slacks? If there is, check the left back pocket, then call me right back."

A few minutes later, the telephone rang and it was Aunt Lou. "Dick, I just can't believe it. The pants are there. And in the left back pocket I found five $100 bills. How could you possibly know the money was there?"

"I didn't know. It almost seems that you've had an authentic message from Uncle Frank." After thoroughly interrogating Frances, I was firmly convinced that she had had no prior knowledge whatever of that $500 in Uncle Frank's pants pocket. How do you explain this phenomenon? I can't.

Another incident that merits telling is this: One afternoon several years ago, my daughter Lynn and I were playing the Ouija board in the recreation room. We were sitting on a davenport about ten feet from a large bar with a formica top. Sentences were being spelled out by the planchette, such as, *I was a whale.*

Then Lynn asked, "What is your name?"

Dutch, was the reply.

"In what country did you live?" I asked.

Third, it spelled.

Other trivial and nonsensical data came through. Then I asked, "Are spirits really guiding our hands on this board?"

The planchette had been making circular movements in the middle of the board. Now it stopped. For perhaps two full minutes it didn't move. We were just about to call it a day when the planchette streaked to *yes.*

Lynn said her fingers were tingling. So were mine. We both felt that a new force, or energy, had moved the planchette under our fingertips.

An idea occurred to me. I asked, "If there is really a spirit guiding our fingers on this board, will you please knock three times on the bar?" The planchette stopped.

We looked over at the bar, but nothing happened. There were no knocks. Nothing.

I repeated the question a little differently. "If you do not knock three times on the bar, we will know there are no spirits in this room."

To our astonishment, we heard three loud knocks on the bar. Lynn emitted a yell of fright and shot out of the room. I stayed where I was, but a cold chill traveled up my spine.

Now just a minute, I thought. There had to be a natural explanation for those raps. Of course! That was it! John must have sneaked into the room. He was hiding behind the bar over there and he had obliged us with the three knocks.

Laughing, I got up and walked over behind the bar. "Come on out, Johnno, I know you're back there. And you know you scared the wits out of your sister."

There was no answer.

"John," I said. "Where in the Sam Hill are you?"

He wasn't there. I examined every inch of space behind the bar, thinking I might find a hidden microphone and speaker that he had set up.

Nothing was there. Chill number two crept up my spine.

How do I explain it? I can't. Was it poltergeist activity? Perhaps. Lynn was about twelve years old at the time.

The next episode I will relate could have a poltergeist overtone. On this occasion, Lynn and a girlfriend, both aged thirteen, were sitting on the davenport in the family room of our new house. The Ouija board was on their knees. The cardboard case for the board, 2½ feet long, was lying on the davenport next to Lynn. I was sitting at the kitchen bar, reading a magazine, about 20 feet away from the girls.

Suddenly I heard a sharp intake of breath from both of the girls. I turned around to look at them. Their eyes were wide and their mouths were open, ready to scream . . . And scream they did, as the cardboard container for the Ouija board ascended from the davenport straight up to about six inches below the ceiling, then floated slowly in my direction.

Just as I realized that my mouth also was open, the case dropped to the floor.

The girls ran from the room, screaming, and their screams brought Dorothy running. "Now what have you done, Richard?" she asked. "Chasing spooks again?"

When I explained what had happened, Dorothy had some practical suggestions.

"Is the damper closed in the fireplace?" It was.

"There must be some windows open in the room here." There were not.

"It must have been a draft from the basement door which must be open." The door was not open.

"Well, then," Dorothy asked, "how could the Ouija board case possibly float through the air and land on the floor way over here?"

I had no explanation at that time. Were the three of us hallucinating? I don't think so.

I related these incidents to an acquaintance who claimed great knowledge on the subject of occultism. He said, "One of you, probably your daughter, unconsciously produced an invisible energy force which resulted in the raps on your bar and the levitation of the Ouija board cover.

"Recently on television, a young Israeli, Uri Geller, stopped the watches of viewers and bent keys in their pockets, simply by extreme mental concentration. Of course, Geller's feats were done consciously whereas your daughter's were subconscious. Nevertheless, the same kind of unknown energy was being used.

"Think about this, Dick—is it not reasonable to assume that the discovery of energies associated with psychic events will be more important than the discovery of atomic energy?"

22

Experiences with OOBE

When our priorities happen to conflict, how often we say, "I can't be in two places at the same time." Yet, according to many researchers, and also several distinguished scientists, you *can* be in two places at the same time. This interesting phenomenon has several names. Among them are: OOBE (out of-body experiences), Bilocation, and Astral Projection.

Several years ago, when my wife and I were serving as cruise directors and dance instructors on a liner sailing to the South Pacific, we met a delightful couple, Mr. and Mrs. Sanders, from Australia. They lived in Canberra, New South Wales. Mr. Sanders was a high government official, and his wife was a concert pianist of considerable fame. At mealtimes they were sitting at the table where Dorothy and I were hosts. One evening at dinner Mr. Sanders told a fascinating story. It is a classic example of OOBE, or Astral Projection.

As Sanders told it, he and his secretary, a Mr. Kent, were returning to Australia by ship after an official trip. They were occupying a two-berth stateroom. Sanders was in the lower berth, Kent in the upper. The weather was very bad. One ship had already been reported lost at sea; and Mrs. Sanders, more than three thousand miles away, grew more and more worried about her husband's safety aboard his homeward-bound ship. One night in bed, she tossed and turned, tormented by her fears, until five o'clock in the morning, desperately wishing there were some way in which she could get in touch with her husband.

Then, as she subsequently described it, she suddenly felt herself leave her body. She felt herself hurtling through the air at tremendous speed toward her husband's storm-tossed ship. That same night, lying wakeful in his lower berth, Mr. Sanders suddenly had the vivid surprise of seeing his wife, wearing only her nightgown, open the door to the stateroom.

He saw her hesitate there a moment, when she caught sight of Mr. Kent in the upper berth. But she came in, and hurried to her husband's side. She bent over him and lovingly stroked his head. Then, not having spoken a single word, she left as quickly and silently as she had come.

In the morning, Kent jokingly asked Sanders who the woman was who had visited him the previous night. Questioning his secretary thoroughly, Sanders discovered that Kent had also been awake, and had seen Mrs. Sanders in the stateroom. Kent said that the clock on the stateroom dresser had shown exactly three o'clock when Mrs. Sanders was there.

The ship reached port safely, and Sanders returned home. His wife's first words to him were, "Do you know that I visited you on the ship?"

"Yes, I do," he said. "But I don't know how you did it, my dear. That night we were more than three thousand miles at sea."

Mrs. Sanders described to her husband her sensations of floating out of her body, speeding airborne over the turbulent seas, and going into the ship and into his stateroom. She was perfectly convinced that what had happened to her was no accident, but a willed action, brought about by her desperate concern for his safety. She knew that the sensation of astral travel had come to her at exactly 5:00 a.m., Australian time; and, like Kent, she had seen the clock in her husband's stateroom showing 3:00 a.m.—which was the proper difference for the ship's location three thousand miles away.

She described the ship, the furniture in the stateroom, and Sanders in the lower berth and Kent in the upper. She remembered her feeling of embarrassment at Kent's awakening to see her in her nightgown.

This report cannot be written off as simply dreams, induced by the mutual deep concern of two loving people. How could Mrs. Sanders know, in a dream, what her husband's stateroom on the ship looked like? How could Kent, as well as Sanders himself, have experienced her visit with such accuracy, if it had only been dreamed? And how, except by actually seeing the clock in the stateroom, could both Kent and Mrs. Sanders have stated three o'clock in the morning as the time when Mrs. Sanders had been there in the stateroom?

Probably all of us at some time have had, in a dream, the sensations of floating. Is this really a dream, or does the soul actually go wandering? Several well-known psychologists put the number of people who have experienced astral projection as high as one in a hundred.

It happens that I can give a first-hand report on a self-induced astral projection, which a young acquaintance of mine performed in my presence. I will call him Hugh (which of course is not his real name). Hugh is the son of friends whom I have known for many years.

What I am going to describe came about in the following way. A college president from Ohio, Dr. Albey, was a friend of my father's. Some years ago, Dr. Albey was a house guest of my parents. One morning I went over to have breakfast with them, and to visit with Dr. Albey.

I liked and respected him very much, but there was one subject on which we always struck sparks from each other. That was the field of psychic phenomena. We always engaged in arguments about this when we met. That morning at breakfast we had a spirited discussion. As usual, neither of us would yield an inch to the other—with one exception.

That exception was OOBE—out-of-body experiences. On this one aspect of psychic phenomena we did partially agree.

That morning, Dr. Albey heatedly declared that actual out-of-body experiences simply do not occur. I said, "Well, perhaps you are right. I do lean toward your thinking in this one matter. But—perhaps we are wrong. I've just had an idea. I know a family here in Portland, whose son was recently discharged from a drug-treatment clinic. Though his cure was effected in a rather bizarre manner, to everyone's amazement the young man recovered. He is anxious to demonstrate what he can do on his drugless trips. So if you are interested," I said, "I'll call him and ask if he would like to be tested tonight. He claims that when he is in a hypnagogic state his secondary body can travel to any place he desires. Furthermore, he says he will describe locations, people, and weather conditions, and in some cases he will relate what people have said even if they are ten thousand miles away from his hypnagogic body."*

As Dr. Albey was interested, I telephoned to Hugh, who was elated at the prospect. His parents were at the coast for the weekend, he said. They would be sorry they had missed out on the fun, and they would be especially sorry not to meet the well-known Dr. Albey. Hugh said he would expect us at his house about eight o'clock that evening. With this

---

*Between wakefulness and sleep.

arranged, Dr. Albey now called a friend in Columbus, Ohio, and talked at some length in what I took to be Chinese. When he hung up, I asked him about this.

"Yes, Dick," he said, "I was speaking to an old friend who was a fellow student with me at Tunghai University on Taiwan many years ago. I was a Rhodes scholar, one of the Oberlin grads in an exchange program for the study of Asian cultures, and this friend and I were roommates at the university. I telephoned him just now, to arrange a plan with him for this evening. In Columbus, the time is three hours ahead of us here in Portland. And so, at 12 o'clock this evening, Eastern time, my friend will be at a certain place. He will pick a certain book out of a bookshelf and examine it briefly, and then he will talk with another person who will be in the room."

Dr. Albey held out a pad of paper. "On this paper," he said, "I am going to write, in Chinese, a detailed description of the location, and of what will be said there. I will then put the paper in an envelope which I will seal. I will leave the envelope in your car until our experiment is over. In my mind, there is absolutely no possibility that your friend Hugh will know any of the content of that envelope." Dr. Albey proceeded to put his plan on paper.

Now let me supply some background on Hugh. To his parents' great anxiety and grief, Hugh had been one of those unfortunate young people who deteriorate into hard-drug addicts, and it had looked as if he had thrown away a promising future. For two years he had been incarcerated in a well-known drug-rehabilitation clinic on the east coast, but he had not responded to the conventional treatment given to hard-drug addicts; and hope for his recovery had gone steadily downhill. By that time, the hospital staff was calling him "Hopeless Hugh," in tragic reality.

When this nadir had been reached, one of the doctors in the clinic asked permission to experiment on Hopeless Hugh, with an unorthodox psychic theory. The hospital board did not accept this theory; but since Hugh's case had now been determined to be incurable anyway, the board gave its permission for the doctor's experimentation. Hugh's parents gave their permission also, and the doctor undertook the program he had in mind.

This was to induce an altered state of consciousness in the boy by using astral projection, in lieu of the drug-induced trips which had nearly destroyed him. The doctor had done extensive and thorough study on this subject, using such books as Sylvan Muldoon's *The Projection of the Astral Body*, Robert Crookall's *The Study and Practice of Astral Projection and More Astral Projections*, and Oliver Fox's *Astral Projection.*

Contrary to the expectations of everyone except this doctor, the experimentation was successful, and Hugh was able to return to his parents' home in Portland. However, the doctor told Hugh's parents that there still remained the possibility of a small problem which might somewhat delay the boy's complete recovery and total return to normality. This possible problem was that Hugh had become psychologically addicted to OOBEs, and therefore had no desire to terminate his astral trips. He had become exceedingly knowledgeable in this matter, and was now looking for opportunities to give demonstrations and prove his abilities. Because his parents had told me the whole story, I had been waiting with much interest for a chance to participate in what sounded to me like a very exciting thing to watch.

Now here was the chance. At eight o'clock that evening, Dr. Albey and I were ringing the front doorbell at Hugh's house. Hugh greeted us with pleasure and escorted us up to his big bedroom. There we settled down to talk about astral projection. It soon became clear that Hugh had indeed accumulated an extensive theoretical knowledge of OOBEs. He sounded like a veritable encyclopedia on the subject.

"There are several ways of voluntarily leaving the body," he said. "One way is to relax completely and concentrate on each part of your physical body. The next step is to will your secondary or spirit body to release itself from each successive point of concentration. Also concentrate on the top of your head, where the secondary body will exit by means of an imaginary trap door. Researchers in this field say that the majority of persons who experience spontaneous OOBEs report the sensation of leaving the body through the top of the skull."

Since Dr. Albey and I were an attentive audience, Hugh warmed to his subject. "Another method is to get the secondary body to carry out an act which the physical body cannot perform. The experimenter should go to sleep hungry or thirsty. Then the secondary body might project in order to meet this physical need. During this experiment the subject must lie on his back, and remain emotionally calm.

"One of the most difficult methods," Hugh went on, "deals with the use of will power. First you must breathe deeply, then project all thought to the top of the skull. Alternate between tensing and relaxing your scalp muscles, then your facial muscles, neck muscles, upper arms, and so on, down your entire body to your toes. Next you must concentrate on your heart, until your whole body feels its pulsation. When this is mastered, you must learn to become aware of pulsations in any part of your body. Next you must learn to control the speed of your heartbeat. When you have learned to make it steady and very slow, an OOBE will occur without conscious willing."

Hugh was clearly enjoying his role as a lecturer. "Still another method is to stare at your own image in a mirror, and attempt to convince your conscious mind that the mirror image is the real self. You will gradually fall asleep doing this exercise. Another method is to concentrate your attention on mental images of light, then imagine yourself as a point floating in space. Other images can also be used, such as the image of swirling out of the body, or images of cones passing through a waterspout and passing through the hole in the side of a thick steel tank. One researcher says that in order to produce OOBEs effectively, you must eat no nuts or meat, and limit your diet to fruit and vegetables, concentrating especially on raw eggs, carrots and liquids.

"My first OOBE," said Hugh, "occurred when I was lying on my hospital bed one afternoon, half awake. Suddenly I heard a faint rushing noise in the far distance. Then it became louder and louder, until I thought my eardrums would burst. I tried to get out of bed, but I found myself cataleptic. Exerting every ounce of energy I had, finally I was able to move my head, and this brought me out of the trance. Later in the week this experience again occurred, only this time in the middle of the night. I saw disembodied heads all around me; their lips were moving but I could hear nothing. This was unpleasant. But it wasn't half as bad, I can tell you, as some of the heroin trips which I would have liked to abort but couldn't!"

Hugh took a luxurious deep breath and went on. "Another technique is using the dream state as a method of projecting. If, during a dream, you are aware that you are dreaming, you can often will yourself awake, and find yourself projected. Sometimes projection occurs in the borderline state between waking and sleeping. This state is called hypnagogic. It's similar to daydreaming. This state is the one in which I can do my most effective projections—I'll prove this to you, a little later on. Oh, yes, and there is one other method of projection that is often used; it has to do with breathing techniques, especially those involved in holding the breath. I have not had much success, myself, with this method.

"Now," said Hugh, "let me warn you...I agree with Robert Crookall, who believes that conscious experimentation with astral projection is very dangerous—not because demon possession or death might occur, but because of physical and psychological perils. For example, certain breathing exercises, such as holding the breath, can disturb blood pressure and put excessive stress on the heart. Staring into a mirror for a long period of time often causes dissociation and psychotic disorders. Conscious control of the heartbeat often causes fibrillations. Other techniques can actually cut off the oxygen supply to the brain. But if you have had a predisposition to the experience of OOBE from the time you were a child, by all means continue your experimenting! Or if you make the mistake of becoming addicted to hard drugs, as I did, try to find a therapist who can teach you projection as a substitute. Believe me, it works!"

Hugh stopped and gave us his happy smile. "Well, I've talked long enough. Are you ready for your little experiment, Dick?"

"Almost," I replied. "Do you mind, Hugh, if I first have a little conference with Dr. Albey in the next room?"

"Not at all," he said. "But don't leave. I'm going to run down to the corner store and will be back in ten minutes."

As soon as Hugh left, I asked Dr. Albey, "What did you write on the paper in the envelope? My curiosity is getting the better of me!"

He shook his head. "Sorry, Dick. If Hugh might be able to pick up any of what I wrote, I would prefer that only one of us has the information. I'm not an exponent of mind-reading—frankly I don't believe in it. Nevertheless I try to keep an open mind."

I smiled at him. "Not at breakfast this morning, Doctor," I reminded him.

"You will recall we were arguing about a different matter," he said. "Mediums, I believe. You certainly are intelligent enough to realize that all mediums are fraudulent. Furthermore, I'm here tonight just to please your dad—I know he is somewhat interested in the paranormal."

He stopped, and then made another start. "No, truthfully my real reason in coming with you tonight is to prove to you that astral projection is just as fraudulent as the seance room."

I wasn't going to get into another argument right then. "Well now, Dr. Albey," I said, "you may be right. But on the other hand we might both have a surprise in store for us tonight."

"Very unlikely, Dick," he snorted.

At this point, Hugh returned, and we settled down again. Hugh stretched out on the bed, lying on his back, and said, "It will take about five minutes for me to go under. I may or may not say anything when I'm hypnagogic. As soon as I come out, I'll give you a complete description of where I've been and what I've seen and heard. Now, Dr.Albey, will you give me the number, street, city and country where you wish me to visit?"

"1411 State Street South, Apartment 22A, Columbus, Ohio, U.S.A.," Dr. Albey replied promptly.

We both began to watch Hugh intently. His breathing was slow and even, and his eyes remained open. After two or three minutes, his eyes seemed to glaze.

I nudged Dr. Albey. "Notice his eyes!" I whispered.

"Yes, there's a change," he whispered back.

For the next half hour, Hugh did not move a muscle. Dr. Albey's head began to nod, and the next thing I knew, he was snoring softly. My own eyes were closed. I was almost asleep, myself.

"Dick," came Hugh's voice.

I sat up with a jerk. Hugh was sitting up on the edge of his bed, smiling.

"How long have you been awake, Hugh?" I asked.

"Just got back," he replied. "You had better wake Dr. Albey. I have some interesting information for him."

I cleared my throat loudly and shifted my weight on the davenport where we were sitting together. Dr. Albey's eyes popped open. "Sorry!" he exclaimed. "I drifted away. Well, Hugh, what do you have to tell us?"

"Dr. Albey," said Hugh, "I have been in a most beautiful apartment. The furniture was predominantly Oriental. Next to the front door was a hutch about six feet high. Exquisite carvings with inlaid mother-of-pearl graced the sides of the piece. On the top shelf there was a Ming vase about eight inches tall. On the base of the vase is a small crack running horizontally, about half an inch long."

I glanced at Dr. Albey. His lips were tight and compressed. His color was ashen. Well, well, I thought, so Hugh really does have a "double" who goes on expeditions!

In a faint voice, Dr. Albey asked, "Who was in the room? Can you describe them?"

"Yes," said Hugh. "When I first entered the room, I saw a tall Oriental gentleman looking at the books in the bookcase with the glass doors. He opened one of the doors—which pulled up and then pushed back into the case—and took out a book. It was small and green, and it had gold lettering on the binding edge. It was entitled *The Poems of Alfred Tennyson, Volume I, 1830-1856*. He opened the book to page 195. At the top of the page was "Locksley Hall." He read the following lines aloud:

'Til the war-drum throbb'd no longer, and the battle flags were furl'd
In the Parliament of man, the Federation of the world.
There the common sense of most shall hold a fretful realm in awe,
And the kindly earth shall slumber, lapt in universal law.

"This Oriental gentleman (he looked Chinese)," said Hugh, "then put the book on a coffee table that was made entirely of glass. On its surface embedded in the middle of the glass was a pastoral scene...sheep grazing, a lake, and a snow-capped mountain in the distance."

I looked at Dr. Albey again. Now his lower lip was trembling, and he was clenching and unclenching his hands. In a hoarse whisper he said, "Yes, you must have been there, Hugh. Now who else was in the room?"

"An older Oriental lady," said Hugh, "rather heavy-set and short. She was wearing a short red gown with a white fur collar...oh yes, she was sitting on the high-backed chair, and there were crutches next to her. Her right leg was in a cast up to her knee."

Dr. Albey's whisper could scarcely be heard now. "Did they say anything?"

"Yes," said Hugh. "They talked about living in the United States. They liked it. They called it the beautiful country. Then the gentleman said, 'The beautiful county is kind to the stranger, but the heart of the wanderer yet yearns for the land of his home.'"

Dr. Albey groaned and put his head in his hands. "That's enough," he said. "This is all correct. It's all down on the paper in Dick's car, written in Chinese. I just can't understand how you get this," he said to Hugh. "Will you please give me the names of books on this subject? I have much reading to do."

23

The Human Aura

The existence of the aura is a scientific fact. The aura is a special atmosphere that surrounds the human body, just as an atmosphere surrounds our Earth. It may be felt as heat, or smelled as odor, and this we experience daily. Psychics and clairvoyants are often able to see the aura; and under certain conditions it can be sensed by sight by nearly everyone.

Evidence of the human aura can be found in the historical records of the most ancient mystics. The elaborate headdress of the Egyptian, and the nimbus of the Christian saint, represent auras. The halo seen in the paintings of Christ is very likely intended as a representation of His aura. Several unique individuals who were fortunate enough to have natural aura-vision have left such unusual records of the aura and its significance that science was finally moved to investigate it.

One fascinating report is the following: A woman with natural aura-vision was on one occasion waiting for an elevator in a department store. When the elevator stopped and the door opened, this woman recognized instantly that everyone inside the car had lost his aura. Alarmed, she refused to enter the car. In addition she urged all the occupants to leave it. But her pleading was ignored by everyone. The door closed and the elevator started. Just moments after that, the elevator cable snapped. The car crashed to the bottom of the shaft, and all the passengers were killed.

Science now postulates that the aura is a field of electromagnetic energy. Research in the field of bioelectric phenomena has indicated that all forms of life—animal and plant—are surrounded by auras, yet, up to the present, very little dependable research on the human aura has been conducted. Therefore, this is a wide-open field, to which amateur investigators may be able to make substantial contributions.

Researchers in England have found that the human aura appears as a triple-decked envelope surrounding the human body. Next to the skin is a narrow dark band, about a quarter-inch wide. Outside this dark band is a second layer called the *inner aura*. This is from two to four inches thick, and it is the clearest of the three layers. Outside this inner aura is the third layer, the *outer aura*. It is misty in aspect, and it lacks a sharp outline at the outer edge. This outer aura is usually about six inches wide. Normally, fugitive radiations, which are continually moving and changing, can be seen darting out at right angles from the body.

People who are able to see the human aura say that it is a pulsating, moving thing. It may have one color, it may have many. Apparently the colors vary with the emotions or thoughts of the person. But the color combinations are never static; they continually pulsate and change.

The second layer, or inner aura, is nearly colorless, although always faintly colored—sometimes light green, or gold, or silver. This inner aura has been described as similar to heat waves shimmering up from a city street on a very hot day. The visible colors are in four bands, beginning just outside the inner aura, with one color usually predominating.

Modern research on auras was initiated by a medical scientist who felt that through the aura there might be dramatic diagnostic possibilities. Inasmuch as body heat is a positive index of physical health, and the aura is at least partially created by body heat, it seems reasonable that changes in the aura may indeed indicate changes in physical health. In fact, it is believed that the breakdown of the aura can forecast illness, long before physical symptoms are observed.

Aura researchers have found that organic diseases seem to affect the first and second auras—the two inside ones—and that the outer aura is affected by nervous diseases. The aura's general shape seems to indicate the presence of disease—if any disease is present. Physical ailments appear to cause changes in the brightness of the aura; and nervous ailments are indicated by changes in the quality of its colors.

Investigators of the human aura have observed rays of light coming from the body. Many clairvoyants have seen these rays emanating from members of a circle of sitters in a seance room, or moving from person to person, or from a person to an object in the room.

Later it was determined that such a person was thinking about the other individual or about the object contacted by the rays during the seance, at the same time that the rays were seen by the clairvoyant. It therefore appears that such rays are a result of directed consciousness. Some researchers think that the rays are a means of communication between this world and the next.

Before the human eye is able to see the aura in color, it must have proper conditioning. Special goggles for this purpose can be purchased. Such goggles have tinted lenses which obscure the red and orange rays and emphasize the violet colors, since the light of the aura is believed to be ultraviolet.

With practice it is possible for the naked eye to see the first two layers of the aura—the two inside ones. But no colors will be visible to you unless you happen to be one of those rare, gifted individuals who have naturally conditioned eyes. And even to be able to see the colorless aura around a human head, the background must be dark and the light in the room not too bright.

In effect, what you should do is try to "glaze" your eyes and look toward the head, but not directly at it. Then you may have to stare for several moments before you see the line, slightly above the head and following its contour. When you succeed in doing this, you are experiencing *aura-vision*, which is limited to the inner aura, almost colorless. The more you practice, the easier it will be for you to see auras, even when lighting and background conditions are not ideal.

Several years ago, I wished to sell one of our automobiles, so I ran an ad in the newspaper. In a few days a lady responded to the ad. She came to inspect the car, and said she would buy it. We agreed to meet at her bank the next day, when she would give me a cashier's check in exchange for my title to the car.

We met next day at the bank. As we talked, we were leaning on a counter which faced an area where a number of men and women were working at their desks. At that time, I had just recently learned to see auras under poor lighting conditions, and I was pleased to be able to observe aura lines around all the heads in the area. Oh-oh, I thought, all of a sudden. There is a strange one—the young man who is sitting at the third desk seems to have a big bump in his aura above his forehead! I wonder what that means.

"Mr. Walker," said my car-purchasing friend, in a soft voice, "I see that you are looking at the young man with the large bump in his aura. That young man will not be alive next week at this time."

Good heavens, I thought, is this lady a mind-reader, or can she really see that bump in his aura? At any rate, she must certainly be mistaken. That young man can't be a day over twenty-five, and to me he looks exceptionally robust.

"So you can see auras, too?" I said to her.

"Yes," she said, "and I can see and interpret aura colors. I know you don't believe me, Mr. Walker, but that young man with the bump in his aura will have a fatal heart attack before the week is over." Our conversation was interrupted by the cashier, who presented me with the check.

"I'm late for an appointment and I must run now," said the new owner of my old car, shaking hands with me. "Oh, one last thing, Mr. Walker. The price I paid for the car was very fair, but you forgot to tell me that you had to have the battery charged twice this week, and it will probably have to be replaced."

Thunderation, I thought, she's right! I was going to warn her about that battery, but it completely slipped my mind. Well, as I suspected, she was a clairvoyant. However, she was certainly wrong about one thing. In order to make doubly sure, I turned to the cashier who had just given me the check.

"Is the young man at the third desk in good health?" I asked.

The cashier laughed. "Indeed he is! He is the captain of our softball team, and he jogs two miles every morning before he comes to work."

The following week I found myself driving in the neighborhood of the bank, though I had no idea why. As long as I was there, I thought I might as well go in and see if that fellow still had the bump in his aura. The third desk was empty. I looked around for the cashier who had given me the check. He was nowhere in sight, so I walked over to the bank guard who was standing close by.

"Where is the young fellow who sits at the third desk over there?" I asked him.

"Bill Stevenson?" said the guard. "Oh, his funeral was yesterday. He had a heart attack and died right there at his desk. And only twenty-four years old. He was the captain of our softball team, you know."

24

Healing via Aura

"You've got to meet this fellow," said my friend Stan, with enthusiasm. "He heals you by working on your aura. He's a truck driver by trade, but when he is not driving his truck, he's patting people's auras back into shape. And believe me it's absolutely miraculous what he can do!"

"What do you mean, patting auras back into shape?" I asked.

"Well," said Stan, "first of all, this man has perfect aura-vision. If you have a disease, or if your have been injured, this truck driver can tell you the exact location of your ailment or injury by examining your aura. He maintains that the aura will be out of shape, or will even have a hole in it, at the site of the ailment. Then without even touching your body, he normalizes your aura by patting and kneading it back into its proper shape. It's sort of a ridiculous sight," continued Stan, "to see Keith work on a patient. If you didn't understand what he was doing, you would surely think he was a prime candidate for a mental institution, as he furiously pats and kneads the air a couple of inches above the patient's body."

I couldn't help saying, "Stan, you used the right word a minute ago—ridiculous!"

"Now wait a minute, Richard! Aren't you the guy who advocates the open-mind policy? I've *seen* Keith heal by working on the aura, and I tell you it's nothing short of miraculous!"

"What does he charge? Five dollars a treatment?" I asked.

"No, sir, one dollar, that's all."

"Ah," said I. "Here's another one practicing medicine without a license. Well, it's a cinch he's not going to get rich, unless he's treating a couple of hundred people a day! Okay, Stan, I'll re-open my mind, and I will invest a dollar in your aura-doctor. As a matter of fact, I do have a slight health problem. But I'm not going to tell you what it is, so you won't accidentally tip off your Dr. Keith."

"I wouldn't do that, Richard, and you know it!" Stan protested. "All right, then, I'll call and see when you can get an appointment. I warn you, he's a very busy fellow. You would be surprised how many prominent local citizens go to him for treatment."

Stan called me later at my home, and said, "Can you make it next Friday at 5:30 p.m.? And I'll meet you there, if you don't mind. I want to see your reaction to this amazing fellow." I had the time free, and Stan gave me Keith's address.

The fact was, a throbbing tooth had just sent me to see my dentist. X-rays showed an abscess which, he had told me, could only be corrected by root-canal therapy. He explained the root-canal procedure, and made an appointment for me to return the following week.

The discomfort from the abscess was most distressing. But, for me, the anticipation of the remedial action which my dentist had described was little short of terrifying. My aversion to tools of the dental profession is almost patholog-ical. At the prospect of this root-canal project, I seriously contemplated going through the rest of my life with a throbbing tooth, rather than honor next week's appointment.

Meanwhile, Friday arrived. Although my face was not swollen, the pain from the tooth had not diminished. If Stan's aura-doctor friend could relieve this pain, I promised myself I would give him a generous tip.

Stan met me at Keith's place, as planned, and he introduced us to each other. A small, muscular man in his early forties grasped my hand cordially. For a moment the pain from his powerful grip on my hand overshadowed the pain from my tooth.

"Sit down, Dick," said Keith. He pushed me onto a stool. Then he backed off a few feet and studied my contours with narrowed eyes.

"You're in pretty good shape," he said at last, "except . . . wow! You must have an awfully sore tooth there!" He shook his head sympathetically. "There's a hole in your aura by your upper lip, under that mole on your cheek. And the color! I'm not going to tell you about the color! Well, I can fix this easy."

Incredible! He had pinpointed the spot exactly. My dentist had said it was my second molar, which is right under the mole on my check.

"Now don't be alarmed, Dick," said Keith. "I'm going to get your aura back in shape for you, and get the right color back."

With great gusto he started patting, kneading, and stroking—about three inches above my face. If I had felt better, I would certainly have laughed at this ludicrous sight of an adult male performing in such an idiotic manner. After three or four minutes, with perspiration streaming down his face, he stopped his frantic hand-jive and said, "I've repaired the hole, and the right color is coming back. You should be all right now."

Stan had been intently watching this imbecilic-appearing treatment, his face wreathed in delighted smiles. Now he exclaimed, "What did I tell you, Dick? Isn't it amazing! You've been healed!"

Well, the tooth had indeed suddenly stopped throbbing, but I wasn't going to become ecstatic. Not just yet. What was going to happen, I wondered, if I touched it with my tongue? Recent experience with that had produced a decidedly unpleasant reaction.

I had to find out. My tongue lightly touched the tooth, while I held my breath...no pain! Very cautiously I tapped the tooth with my fingernail. . . no pain!

What an outstanding coincidence, I thought. Or was it a coincidence? The pain had certainly ceased, the moment Keith stopped his frantic hand movements and announced that he had repaired the hole in my aura. But my dentist had told me that he would have to drill a small hole to the abscess, so that it would drain. Then, he said, he would remove the nerve from the offending tooth. Probably he might even have to remove the roots also. The entire procedure would not be pleasant, he had told me frankly, yet it was the only way the pain could be alleviated.

Well, I thought, still being cautious, perhaps I was experiencing only a brief moratorium from the pulsating torment of the abscess. Just the same, the relief was enormously welcome, even if temporary. I pressed a $5 bill into the palm of Keith's hand.

"My fee is one dollar, and I accept no tips," he said. He produced four $1 bills and shoved them into my pocket.

The following week, I was still rejoicing in my pain-free condition. I called my dentist and told him to cancel my root-canal appointment as I was no longer in pain. Apparently the abscess had gone away.

"Impossible!" he said. "If you don't get in here soon, you'll be sorry!"

I did not go down, however. Then, several weeks later I bit down on a hard piece of candy, and a crown fell off. I called the dentist and made an appointment to get it cemented back on.

"While you are here, I'm going to X-ray that abscessed second molar," he said, when I got down to the office. He proceeded with the X-rays and their development, and brought them to the chair.

"Look here!" he told me. "There is absolutely no sign of the abscess...that tooth is totally healthy! I don't understand it."

I smiled at him. "Doctor, you may recall that I was very reluctant to go through with that root-canal procedure you so graphically described to me. Therefore, I suspect that the Omnipotent took pity on me and arranged for a spontaneous healing."

"Very amusing, Richard," he said, not at all amused. "But I wish I knew what really happened to that abscess." I didn't have the heart to tell him that he had been upstaged by a truck-driving aura-doctor.

The USSR and the Soviet-bloc countries are pouring time, scientific talent, and large sums of money into parapsychological research—including extensive studies on the human aura. The results are astounding new knowledge in every area of parapsychology. It is rumored that much of what has been discovered is a closely guarded secret. Also, there is no question that the West is far behind the Communists in the new field of mind research.

One of the many new Soviet inventions is a machine that photographs the human aura. An electrician by the name of Semyon Kirlian, who worked in a research institute in southern Russian near the Black Sea, invented a high-frequency camera-microscope that was able to take pictures of the luminous energy coming from the human body and from every other living object.

One day Kirlian and his wife were taking high-frequency photographs of two leaves which had been removed from different plants of the same species. To their surprise, the photos of the two leaves were entirely different. The luminescence from one leaf had a totally different symmetry than that from the other leaf.

The Kirlians had no way of interpreting this apparent contradiction. The enigma was finally solved by a botanist, who explained that even though both leaves had been removed from the same species of plant, one of the plants had a serious disease. Though the infected plant and leaf showed no physical indication that the plant was infected and would soon die, the Kirlian camera-microscope had demonstrated that it was possible to diagnose plant illness in advance, with high-frequency photographs!

Multicolored flashing lights seen in the pictures appeared to be an *energy counterpart body* of the leaf. Long before a disease could be seen in the physical body of a plant, it existed in the counterpart body of energy. Therefore, if plant disease could be successfully diagnosed before it became visible, perhaps steps could be taken to prevent the disease from developing!

It appears that all living things have two bodies—the material body, and the secondary energy body which can be seen in high-frequency photographs. For centuries, clairvoyants, philosophers and religious figures have spoken of the invisible body which everyone has. This has been called the energy body, the astral body, the etheric body, the Beta body, the spirit body, and so forth.

What about the human body? Could the same diagnostic procedure used on plants be applied to the human body? A scientist in England, using special infrared eyeglasses, reported that he could indeed observe the same phenomena in human bodies. Illness, depression and fatigue affected the human aura, according to this scientist, and he became able to diagnose the condition of the body, according to the colors and shape of the aura.

Researchers in Russia have now perfected new optical instruments so that the Kirlian photography can be hooked up to ultra-powerful electronic microscopes. This amazing high-frequency photographic technique may quite possibly revolutionize research in every area of science and technology.

It appears that all living things not only have a physical body made of atoms and molecules, but also a facsimile body of energy. What generates this energy body, and how can it be replenished?

Soviet scientists found that the oxygen we breathe converts electrons into the energy body. This energy or secondary body (perhaps it should be called the primary body), which reacts to changes in thought and to changes in the environment, might supply clues that are needed for a reasonable examination of many paranormal occurrences such as ESP, "water witching," and psychic healing. A U.S. scientist suggests that the Kirlian photography indicates that psychic healing is accomplished through a transfer of energy from the energy body of the healer to the energy body of his patient.

Some successful healers say that God does the healing. Others say that healing is done by spirits. Still others state that the healing is done by some unknown and undetectable kind of energy. One healer says he doesn't try to heal, but tries to merge with the patient for one moment, to know completely another way of being in the world—a feeling of absolute concern, that we are all one. At this moment, a healing takes place.

It seems that mystics, mediums and physicists are in complete agreement on the concept that there are two ways of being in the universe—there is the world of the many (the everyday common-sense world), and there is the world of the one (the field theory of the universe).* Using this latter concept, the healer welcomes the patient home to the universe. The patient recognizes this at a subconscious level, and at that moment his body's repair mechanism is stimulated to function at its maximum, and healing takes place.

This might be an effective type of healing that is practiced by many individual healers, Christian Science Practitioners, and prayer circles. Another type, on the other hand, represents an effort on the part of the healer to heal, and he does not go into an altered state of consciousness. Instead, a current of energy flows through his hands and is passed through the area of the patient's illness; and this often results in healing. (This might explain the Healer who temporarily regressed Chinky's pain, in Chapter 19.)

---

*The theory that all human beings are part of one universal consciousness.

25

Men in Black

A friend of mine spends a small fortune on cassette tapes. He follows a compulsive urge to tape-record everything. Even when he goes to sleep at night, he leaves a tape recorder on, hoping to record unusual nocturnal sounds and perhaps paranormal voices.

When our American astronauts made their first trip to the moon, some years ago, this friend of mine taped the entire television coverage of that exciting event. After listening to some of the tapes he made, I am reasonably convinced that on this trip, Buzz Aldrin, Neil Armstrong and Michael Collins saw something that has not been generally known and most certainly was not released to the media. It appears that besides mysterious lights, they saw a formation of spaceships. My friend has allowed me to report on some of the material from these tapes of his, provided I will never divulge the source. His reasons for this will be clear a little later on.

As the astronauts were orbiting the moon, one of them called attention to a crater on the surface. Then nothing was heard on the tape but a buzzing sound.

Later in the tape, Buzz Aldrin transmitted to Mission Control at Houston that they could see a brilliant light in the crater—, but whatever name he had given was garbled and could not be understood from the tape. Then Houston was heard on the tape, asking the astronauts to identify the brilliant light. They replied that they could not, because it was too far away, but that there was definitely considerable activity down there.

At this point the conversation abruptly terminated, as if there had been a transmission failure. However, it was quite obvious to the listener that the transmission had been cut off deliberately.

A newspaper printed in Canada, and distributed in both Canada and the United States, apparently subscribes to this view. The paper declared that the transmission "failure" was fabricated, and what the astronauts had seen was actually an armada of spaceships in a crater on the surface of the moon.

This hypothesis may be hard to accept, but the newspaper declared that it had in its possession a taped transcript of the conversation between the astronauts and Mission Control. This conversation was not heard on television or radio, reported the newspaper, because it was censored out of the transmission by a delayed-tape technique which allowed a lag of as much as four or five minutes between Mission Control reception at Houston and the broadcast that goes over the air.

The material which was censored out of the broadcast showed Houston asking urgently for details, and the astronauts replying that whatever they were seeing was enormous, unbelievable, and apparently was in a crater on the moon, as they were looking down at it. The astronauts told Houston they were seeing some "visitors," and that these visitors had evidently been there for some time, judging by the installations—that the visitors were in fact other spaceships, lined up on the far side of the crater edge.

The astronauts said they took three pictures of the spaceships—if that was what they were—but they thought the film may have been fogged. They also told Houston that they had set up mirrors on the moon, as planned, but that they felt whoever was down there would probably either remove or destroy them, the next day. It was evident, on the tapes, that the astronauts were much disturbed or excited; their hands were shaking, and their voices were trembling.

If the whole thing was not a hoax, the ramifications are provocative, to say the least.

One day my tape-recording friend's doorbell rang. His teenage daughter, peeking out of the window, exclaimed, "Hey, Dad, there are three men dressed in black at the front door, and there's a black car parked out in front. Golly, even their neckties are black!"

Her father went to the door and opened it. "Good afternoon," he said. "What can I do for you gentlemen?"

"May we come in and talk with you?" one of the men asked.

"I think not," said my friend. "What is your business with me, please?"

The spokesman said, "You have certain tapes of the Apollo 11 mission, and we would like to have them."

"Who told you about my tapes, and who do you represent?"

"It doesn't matter who told us, and we represent the United States Government," said the spokesman.

They weren't going to get away with that—not with my friend. "Let me see your credentials," said he.

"Not necessary. We want the tapes now!"

To this, my friend replied, "You wait right there on the porch, gentlemen. I'm going to call the F.B.I. office."

At this, the spokesman said, "Sir, we are going to leave now. But I warn you, if you do not destroy the tapes in question, I promise you that great bodily harm will come to you and to your family." And with that they left.

My friend called the local F.B.I. office, and related the incident to the agent who answered the phone. The agent said he would be over within a half hour. He also advised that if the men in black returned, my friend should not answer the door.

"These MIB—Men in Black—are nothing new," the agent said. "For several years our offices throughout the country have been receiving telephone calls, usually from UFO investigators, or from people who genuinely thought they had seen a UFO.

"What happens is the same as what happened to you. These MIB often travel in three's; they sometimes drive black sedans and follow people; they warn them verbally, and they leave notes stating that they know all about their UFO researching or sighting. The implication is that these MIB represent extra-terrestrial spaceships and that they come to warn the UFO investigators to cease and desist, or horrible things will happen to them. For some reason or other," continued the agent, "we have been unable to apprehend any of these Men in Black, although we have come close to it at times."

26

Paranormal Voices

Some scientists now claim that the tape recorder can pick up broadcasts from other dimensions, and there is well-documented evidence that paranormal voices have been tape recorded under the strictest test conditions. To date, scientific evidence points to two astounding conclusions.

The human voice may, in some unknown way, be able to place voices on magnetic tape from a long distance. And, discarnates are actually trying to communicate with us through the electronic medium of tape-recording. The latter conclusion is more acceptable to pioneer voice-phenomena scientists. For further information, see *Breakthrough* by Konstantin Raudive, in the Suggested Reading List at the end of this book.

In the preceding chapter I wrote about a friend who was a compulsive taper. This hobby brought him a number of adventures, and, in a few instances, embarrassment. Once a union shop-steward apprehended him when he was taping a symphony concert. He was forced to erase the tapes, right there at the concert, in the presence of the steward and of his own friends who were sitting with him.

He was able, however, to conceal one cassette; and when he returned home and played the tape back, to his amazement and joy he heard several paranormal voices. When I first heard this tape, I accused him of dubbing in the voices. His sincere indignation convinced me that I was in error. So I listened to the tape again—this time more intently, and with tongue out of my cheek. The orchestra was playing Claude Debussy's *La Mer*. Suddenly I heard, in a definite French accent, "The sea, do you not hear?"

I asked my friend to rewind and then play it back again. "Couldn't it have been someone sitting close to you?" I asked him.

"Impossible. The recorder was on my lap and I was sitting in the seat next to the aisle. Peg (his wife) was sitting next to me."

"Well," I said, "maybe it was someone who was talking as he walked down the aisle to his seat."

"No one walked down the aisle except the usherette," he insisted. "I saw her look at my recorder and frown. She's the one who tipped off the shop-steward. If I'd had any brains I would have hidden the recorder under my seat. Did you notice how clear and loud that voice was? It sounded as if it was talking very close to the microphone. I tell you, Richard, there was no human being talking into that mike on my lap! Now wait, there's more—listen."

He pushed the fast-forward button, and the numbers on the counter flew by until he reached the desired one, and pushed the stop button. Then above the subdued rumbling of the drums in Sibelius's *Symphony in E Minor*, I heard the same French voice say, "Opus 39, first movement, chère."

"Well, what do you think?" asked my friend.

"Whoever it is seems to know something about classical music," I said. "Mighty strange, though, not to be able to see him. Looks like you had an invisible French music critic sitting on your lap."

"Very funny," he said dryly. "Now listen—there's one more. It's at the very end of this tape. This is going to shake you up a little."

"A little" was incorrect! At the sound of the next voice, a titanic chill permeated my entire being. There was no mistaking the voice of one of my best friends, who had died more than thirty years before. Now, on the tape, I heard him clearly say, "What a mess. Train coming. The road sure cost mom! Hey, Dick!" In the background, the Portland Symphony Orchestra was playing his favorite music, Peter Ilyitch Tchaikowsky's *Nutcracker Suite*, Opus 71-A from *Le Casse-Noisette*.

At the age of 16, the three of us were close friends. For obvious reasons, I will not give real names: Tom, whose tape had just given me the shock of my life; Harry, whose voice had just come over the tape; and I. In some circles we were known as the "Foolhardy Three," when we were behind the steering wheels of our fathers' automobiles.

One of our harebrained enterprises was to drive the cars on railroad tracks. At a wide crossing, one of us would guide the car onto the tracks. Then it was necessary to remove about 20 pounds of air from each tire. And then, if we didn't drive more than 35 miles per hour, and if we did not touch the steering wheel, we had no problems.

Usually we checked the train schedules before we embarked on a long drive via railroad track. Then away we would go, over 100-foot-high trestles, through covered bridges, farm lands, mountains and forests. Often our passing would activate the automatic gate device at crossings, and it was with great delight that we observed the incredulous expressions on the faces of the motorists who were waiting for the "train" to go by.

My father's Plymouth sedan had a hand throttle which I would set at 35 miles per hour. I would climb into the back seat and join Tom and Harry. One day, rolling along, we saw a dear old lady working in her garden next to the tracks. The three of us waved at her. She smiled, waved back—and then fainted dead away.

Fearing we might have caused her to suffer a fatal heart attack, we stopped. We contemplated backing up to render assistance; but fortunately we remembered in time, that if we backed the car, it would leave the tracks and we would be in terrible trouble! It was all right, anyway, because the lady soon got up, shaking her fist at us. After that, she picked up her rake and went back to her job, her mouth working. We presumed she was discussing us. Relieved that she hadn't died from the shock we had given her, we drove on.

On another occasion we rode all the way to the beach, on the old Oregon Electric tracks which were on what is now Barbur Boulevard. Somewhere around the area of Newberg, a state policeman spotted us. He turned on his siren, left the highway, and drove furiously across a field in our direction. Obviously he failed to see a gully that was in his path, because to our immense relief his car disappeared and the siren stopped abruptly. The officer soon emerged from the gully, without his car. He shook his fist at us—and *his* mouth was also working. This time we were sure we were being discussed. We waved back in a friendly manner.

By now, you may have an idea of the significance of the words uttered by long-deceased Harry, that were on Tom's tape: "What a mess! Train coming. The road sure cost mom. Hey, Dick!"

On that particular day, we had been blissfully gliding along the tracks in Harry's mother's air-cooled Franklin limo. This beautiful hunk of metal even had jump seats—those little extra seats behind the front seat and in front of the back seat. I was sitting on one of them.

Ahead of us a quarter of a mile we saw a hobo trudging down the tracks. As we got close to him, I said, "Better honk at him, Harry. I don't think he hears us."

Harry honked. The hobo leaped into the air. His mouth opened and remained open.

We stopped beside him. "Would you like a ride?" I asked, and opened the door. "You can sit on the other jump seat. You'll like it here."

"Well, I dunno," he said doubtfully, looking us over. "How do you keep it on the tracks? Oh well, I guess it beats walkin'. Thanks." He got in and sat down on the other jump seat. I immediately regretted making the invitation. This gentlemen had not bathed for some time. Tom and Harry cast sour looks in my direction, while I tried not to breathe—at least until I could get used to the horrible odor which was now sitting next to me.

The Franklin, like Dad's Plymouth, had a hand throttle. Harry set it at 35 miles per hour, and then crawled over the hobo and me, and into the back seat with Tom.

The hobo's open mouth was working (so many mouths seemed to be working when the "Foolhardy Three" were around). Finally some words came out.

"Boys, I don't think my nerves can stand much more of this—ridin' in this car on the railroad tracks, and with nobody behind the wheel. And what really bothers me is there's a train due along here at any time now and it's comin' our way!"

"Impossible," replied Harry. "I checked the train schedule and there's nothin' due along here until 3 o'clock." I looked at my watch and my heart sank. "Harry! It's 3 o'clock right now!"

"Good Lord!" Harry cried. "My watch stopped. I don't think there's a crossing where we can get off, for another 10 miles. Hey, Dick! Did you hear that?"

We certainly did. It was a train's whistle and it was close! We could see only a short section of track ahead, because of the sharp curve in the road bed. Furthermore, we were in a draw, and on both sides of the track the ground rose steeply. Then we saw it—a flat space just in front of us, that might be large enough for a car, if we could get the car off the track in time. Harry shot out of the back seat, grabbed the wheel, and gave it a mighty turn.

The Franklin flew through the air and landed with a sickening jolt in the small flat area beside the track, precisely as the train roared by. I caught a quick glimpse of the engineer's astonished face peering from the cab. Then I closed my eyes and promised the Lord that henceforth I would be an exemplary preacher's son.

Without even thanking us for the ride, Mr. Hobo uttered several obscenities in direct reference to our characters, then strode off down the track. Harry looked the situation over and said, "What a mess!"

He was right. Unless the railroad brought a derrick, there was absolutely no way we could get the car back up on the track. And somehow we didn't feel that the railroad would be inclined to help us out of our predicament. It took us four hours to walk back home, while Harry kept assuring us that his mother would be very understanding about the whole thing. Besides, she had inherited a large sum of money and would never have any financial worries.

But, at that time, when we broke the news to her, I didn't think she was particularly understanding. Harry's substantial allowance, which we all shared, was taken away for a whole month, and he was not allowed to use any other of the family cars for a week. It cost Harry's mother $493.16 to have a road built in to the flat spot by the track in the draw, where the Franklin was waiting.

When tape recorders first appeared on the market, Harry bought one. We did a lot of taping for fun; and today I have in my possession a reel of tape with Harry's voice thereupon. I borrowed Tom's cassette with the paranormal voices, and took both tapes to a high-frequency electronics engineer, for analysis.

The engineer explained to me that voice prints of voices coming from the same source always show identical patterns. The prints are produced by a sound spectrograph, which traces on graph paper the distinctive sound patterns of a person's voice. The voice print is as reliable as a fingerprint in identifying a person. What were the results of the tests in this case? The voice prints on the two tapes are identical.

Some highly regarded scientists in several countries are convinced that these paranormal voices on tape provide proof of personality survival beyond bodily death. The director of the foremost university institute of parapsychology in Germany has made the statement that the voice phenomena are comparable to nuclear fission, in their significance for mankind.

Steinmetz was once heard to say, "If a loved one moves a long distance away from you, is it abnormal or un-Christian to keep in touch? You will most certainly call him on the telephone occasionally, and will rejoice at hearing his voice. It is no different when a loved one dies. You should still wish to keep in touch."

27

Postmortem Survival

What kind of "afterlife" might there be, based upon the findings of psychical research?

Some researchers argue that the postmorten world must be a kind of dream world. They state that when we are asleep, the sensory stimuli are shut off from our consciousness, yet we still have experiences. Even though our sense perception is not operating at this time, something almost identical to sense perception takes place in our dreams. During our waking hours, our image-producing power is usually inhibited by sensory data which serve as the focusing device that permits us to operate efficiently in this material world, prevents us from bumping into things, and keeps us from being in a somnambulatory state. The sensory bombardment blocks off this image-producing power, so that when we are awake we can operate efficiently.

When we are asleep, however, the image-building mechanism, which we all have, is more free to operate. Therefore, in our dream life our image-making mechanism gives us a great many objects of which we are aware, toward

which we direct our thoughts and actions—in our dreams—
and about which we have desires and emotions. These may
be ugly or beautiful, attractive or repugnant. As we all know,
these objects in our dream life do not always behave
according to the laws of physics, but in our dream world this
never bothers us.

When we awaken and look back on the dream, we may
think, "How ridiculous!" But at the time the dream occurs, it
is coherent, and we believe in it. Our personal identity is
retained and though we are unconscious, our identity remains
unbroken. This, researchers contend, is similar to the postmortem world.

It would not be an imaginary world—but a world of
images. This world would be real to its inhabitants, just as our
dreams are real. Nightmares frighten us, and often we wake
up with our heart pounding. If we dream we are falling, we
think we actually are falling. When we awaken, our dream
world seems unreal and is usually quickly forgotten because it
does not fit the context of our physical consciousness. We
tend to believe that only the waking world is real.

Our dream world would seem real if the various criteria of
reality were not imposed upon our consciousness. Perhaps this
would be the case in a postmortem world. We wouldn't have
different criteria upon which to judge the world of images
because we would not be regaining consciousness into a
different reality. We would be existing exclusively in the
postmortem or world of images, which would not seem
foreign to us because there would be no other world to
compare it with, such as our present world that we can
compare to the dream world.

This kind of reality could explain why, in spiritualistic
literature, there are so many references to discarnates with no
bodily substance, who do not believe they are dead. "I can't
be dead," they declare. "There are objects and people here.

I'm at this point in space, and they're over there." With all these conditions of a physical world around him, the discarnate cannot believe he is dead. He doesn't believe he is dead, because the world of images in which he is now existing as a discarnate is just as real to him as was the world of the five senses when he was alive.

I will now interject personal data regarding a discarnate who could not believe he was dead. The following incident is significant because it did not come from spiritualistic literature but from a direct experience.

I am privileged to have a friend who is an internationally famed hypnotist. He is noted and respected in all fields of hypnosis—medical, research, and stage. He is one of the very few who can do age-regression to alleged previous lifetimes. I was fortunate to witness an example of this remarkable talent of Dr. Larry Sinclair's, which culminated in a mind-boggling double-ending.

A friend of mine, George Myland, who is a civil engineer, had just received the results of a vocational guidance test which he had taken two weeks before. He was not pleased, because it had cost him $35 to find out what he already knew—that he was in the wrong field. The test showed that his true aptitudes were not in civil engineering, but rather in some area of business administration, even though he had been earning a better-than-average living, building bridges (overpasses) for the state highway department.

Somehow or other, George had always been more-than-average successful in his bidding for jobs. Many times his bid had been just a little under that of his closest competitor, so his profit quotient was usually a little higher than normal. He always enjoyed working up the bids, but the actual construction of the bridges was a tremendous bore.

His two children would not be ready for college for several years. Further, he had recently inherited $30,000 from an aunt, so he could get by financially for a while even if he changed vocations. But change to what? This question was the reason he had taken the vocational guidance test. Shortly afterwards, we met at a social function and talked about his problem.

"Richard," he said, "I'm just about at the end of my rope. I'm about to bid on three jobs, and with my luck I'll probably get them all. But as you know, I absolutely despise the work. If I don't get out of it immediately, I'm sure I'll have a complete nervous breakdown."

Something clicked in the back of my head. An idea was developing. It was so off-beat though, that I almost hesitated to mention it to him.

"George," I asked, "have you ever been hypnotized?"

"No," he replied.

"If there is a chance we might discover what your major field of endeavor should be, will you consent to hypnosis?"

"I'll try anything!"

"Fine! I'll set up an appointment with Dr. Larry Sinclair, and I'll call you tomorrow morning."

George Myland did not respond to hypnosis easily. As a very interested spectator I marveled at the tremendous effort, talent and patience on the part of Dr. Sinclair, to get George to only the first stage of unconsciousness.

"We have a long way to go, Dick," muttered Sinclair, perspiration streaming down his face.

About two hours later, the exhausted hypnotist appeared satisfied. "Did you bring your tape recorder?" he asked me.

"Sorry, I forgot it," I said.

"We're out of luck, then, because mine is in the shop being repaired. Get that pad and pen on the table over there, and get ready to take notes. I'm going to start the question session now." And he began.

"What is your name?"

"Franklin S. Fenwick," replied the unconscious George.

"What does the S. stand for?"

"Stanley."

"What is your occupation?"

"Accountant."

"Do you like your work?"

"Very much."

"Are you married?"

"Yes."

"What is your wife's name?"

"Marie."

"Do you have children?"

"No."

"Where do you live?"

"San Francisco."

"Your home address?"

"Seven-eighteen Market Street."

"What is the date?"

"March twenty-fourth."

"The year?"

"Nineteen-hundred twelve."

"Do you remember the earthquake?"

"I wish I didn't."

"Were any of your family injured?"

"No."

"Friends or acquaintances?"

"Yes."

"What was the exact date of your death?"

"February second, nineteen-sixteen."

"What do you recall about your death?"

At this question, George became agitated and started to moan. The following is an accurate reproduction from my notes of what he said:

"Where am I? My God, this is a funeral home! Why, there's Mr. Beeson! I know all these people! Good Lord, there's Marie in the other room, and Mom, Shirley and Jim are on the davenport with her. Hey, Marie! Why are you crying? Why don't you answer me?"

At this point George, d.b.a. (doing business as) Franklin S. Fenwick, apparently attempted to shake the shoulders of his wife.

"My hands are going right through you!" he shouted. "This must be an awful dream! Can't you hear me? Whose funeral is this? God, I can walk right through this door even though it's closed! Oh, no! NO! That's me in the casket—and I've got on my new herringbone suit!"

George began to moan again, and then suddenly started striking his head with his fists.

"That's enough!" shouted Dr. Sinclair. "One, two, three!"

George shook his head, and closed his eyes which had been wide open. Then he opened his eyes again and said, "What's been going on? Guess I've been asleep. How come I'm perspiring so?—and you are, too, Doc—your face is all wet! Dick! You have a silly expression on your face, and you are as pale as a sheet. What's been—oh, yes, now I remember. You were going to do some age-regression on me. How did it go?"

"Read you notes to him, Dick," said Dr. Sinclair, "and I'll make comments from time to time."

We went through my notes. George seemed stunned. At last he said, "Let's check the mortuaries in San Francisco, that might have been in business in 1916. You know, I could never buy the Reincarnation theory, but now I'm not so sure."

"It has a lot going for it," murmured Dr. Sinclair.

My letter to the California Funeral Directors' Association was answered promptly. There were four funeral homes in San Francisco now operating, which had been in business in 1916. Their names and addresses were enclosed.

George wrote to each funeral home, inquiring if their records went back to 1916. If so, did they have a service for a Franklin S. Fenwick sometime around the date of February 2 in that year?

Two of the four had kept records going back to this date. Greely and McKlintock's Chapel by the Bay wrote back that on February 5, 1916, a service was performed in their chapel for a Franklin S. Fenwick. No further information could be released unless requested by an immediate member of the family.

George and I were flabbergasted, but Dr. Sinclair was completely unexcited. "In my business, nothing surprises me any more," he told us.

"There is just one more little bit of evidence I would like to have," said George. "I'm going to telephone the Chapel by the Bay. Listen in on the other phone, Dick."

He dialed the number, and the Chapel answered. George asked his question.

"Oh, yes, Mr. Myland," said the person on the other end. "We recently wrote you about the Fenwick service back in 1916, I believe. I think the file is still out. Just a moment, please, I'll check and see if I can answer your question... Hello, Mr. Myland? Yes, I have the information here for you. The name of Mr. Fenwick's wife was Marie. I'm sorry I can't give you any more data unless you are an immediate member of the family."

"Thank you very much," said George, "but I don't wish any further information. Incidentally, I am an immediate member of the family—very immediate. You see, I am the deceased."

There was a gasp on the other end of the line. "Whaaaat? Now really, Mr. Myland—"

Under hypnosis, George Myland had claimed to be an accountant in his previous lifetime. To the question, "Do you like your work?" he had answered, "Very much."

On the basis of this information, plus the fact that he always enjoyed working with figures, George went back to college for two years, majoring in accounting and minoring in mathematics. His grade point average was 4. It is interesting to note that when George Myland had majored in civil engineering, as a college student the first time around, he almost did not get his degree because of poor grades.

Today my friend George Myland is a senior partner in a huge accounting firm. He is supremely happy in his work, and he attributes his success to vocational guidance through hypnotism, and to a certain Mr. Franklin S. Fenwick who had also been an accountant.

Many years ago, when Dr. Larry Sinclair was a young man, he attended a week-long seminar on medical hypnosis. The guest speaker was none other than world-renowned psychologist Dr. Carl Jung. The following is from Dr. Sinclair's notes: One evening after dinner, when Dr. Jung was idly chatting with Larry Sinclair and several other students, he suddenly exclaimed, "Quick! Get paper and pencils and take notes! I'm going into a trance!"

With eyes closed, he began breathing heavily for a couple of minutes. Then he jumped to his feet and raised both arms. An entirely new voice began speaking, completely foreign to his normal German accent.

"Good evening, my friends. I'm pleased to try to speak with you. During the course of our conversation, it will be my happiness to assist you along a seldom-easy path of life. To those of us in our world whose work it is to try to be of service to the earth world, it is our wish and our work to try to further an understanding that it is a place as natural as your world, and it is merely in a different vibration.

"This, we believe, if it could be understood, might assist much in the evolution of character of those still in the body. It is not of much use killing people, when you do not truly kill them. It is not of much use, if you know very well that when you come to our world you will meet those you have done bad things to, on the earth plane. You cannot escape them.

"There can be hazards if you tamper too much with the metaphysics when in the body. Nevertheless, a sensible approach with one foot firmly on the ground can be of tremendous benefit to most people.

"In this particular area of exploration, I would advise you in this manner: Accept the information which is given to you allegedly from our world, that seems to ring true within your heart. Accept also that part of the readings and writings of others, that also seems to ring true within your heart. There are many aspects and many teachings. We who have to use earthly instruments such as this one, have to contend with the mind and the prejudices of that instrument.

"May I give you an example? If you pour oil into a vessel that is shaped round, the oil will be round-shaped in that vessel. Therefore the words we pour through human instruments take the shape of the mind of that instrument, although the essence of that message may well remain.

"And here is our problem. Some instruments are better than others. Psychic gifts are not always spiritual. Rather it is a gift that is like music. Not all of those who are endowed with the gift of music lead lives that are spiritual in nature. We simply have to make use of what material is available."

Dr. Jung—or whoever was using his vocal cords—stopped talking, and Larry Sinclair eagerly asked, "In the next world you are speaking of, is there an actuality that can be related to the actuality here on earth?"

The voice from Dr. Jung's throat replied, "What you ask is, are we able to touch each other? Yes, indeed. Are we made up of physical matter? To each other, yes. Is it not a scientific fact that the material things in your world are not really solid?

They are held together by atoms, molecules, and other units of energy. Our vibrations are much faster than the solid matter in your world. Therefore, you are not solid to us, and we are not solid to you. Of course, when you graduate into our world, to each other you are just as solid.

"Through many sources you may hear many descriptions of our world, and it is probably all true—our world is extremely diverse in character.

"To explain in words what our world is like is impossible. Could a Java Ape Man, drawing a picture in the sand, portray the reality of an airplane? The real image could not be conveyed that easily. As we are multi-dimensional, there are certain aspects of our life that we are not able to give a parallel to.

"I'm able to give you some information. Of course we have no physical ailments, but we do have spiritual illness. Creative impulses are allowed to progress freely, and living is much happier, even though it is not much different from the memories of life on earth."

At this point, Dr. Jung's eyes opened. He looked around the room and then exclaimed, "What have I been saying? Let me see your notes...Aha—just as I thought!" Then reflectively, he said, "I'm afraid my dear old teacher Sigmund Freud would not approve. I'm sure he would say, 'It was only one of your secondary personalities coming through, Carl...don't believe a word of it!'

"Gentlemen, I don't believe the information I have just read from your notes came from one of my secondary personalities. Nevertheless, you may draw your own conclusions. Keep in mind, however—we do not see things as they are, we see things as we are."

28

A Summing Up

What are my conclusions about the strange episodes of which I have written? Nothing absolute, I'm sorry to say—but I do have a theory or two.

First of all, it's doubtful if man's psychic powers can be explained on any material basis. We can measure the results of a psychic process, such as, a greater flow of saliva, increased adrenalin, and so on, but we can't measure the process itself any more than we can measure an idea. I presented this thought to a biologist I know. He dogmatically replied:

"You are wrong. An idea is only an electrical discharge in the brain." My rebuttal was:

"I'll agree that an idea from the mind produces an electrical discharge in the brain, but does that prove they are the same thing? I don't think so. You just can't apply materialistic criteria to this."

A few years ago, I had the good fortune to chat with one of Dr. B. J. Rhine's associates from Duke University's Parapsychology Laboratory. I recall a few of his statements:

"Psychic phenomena can't be understood by objective scientific study. We have to make ourselves receptive to actual paranormal experiences. In this area we can't learn the truth through logic—we have to probe deep into our unconscious to the concealed layers of knowledge. If we can't learn to accept, we can't learn to understand."

It's somewhat difficult for me to believe that spirits, under certain conditions, visit us, produce noise to attract our attention, and even communicate with us through the seance trumpet—although perhaps they do. I'm more inclined to agree with Dr. Charles Richet, a famous French psychical researcher and winner of the Nobel Prize in physiology. He said he couldn't adopt the inference that there are spirits or intelligences outside of human intelligence. He felt that the human personality has both material and psychological powers that we do not know about—and in our present state of knowledge, are not in a position to know about.

On the other hand, the noted French astronomer and psychical researcher, Camille Flammarion, wrote that he was convinced that the manifestations he analyzed proved "there is no death and intelligent forces exist all around us."

So here we have two brilliant scientists researching in the same area with opposing views. As a non-brilliant layman, I believe I can appreciate both opinions, and my conclusions remain in limbo. I do have a thought, however, as to how all of this phenomena is produced:

We now know that the unusual incidents occurring in the seance room are the result of ectoplasm flowing from the medium's body. This phenomenon has been observed by researchers in broad daylight as well as in a dark room through infrared eye glasses.

I am suggesting that from his subconscious mind, the medium's secondary personality is directing the ectoplasm's activities. Or, perhaps, discarnates are able to communicate with us through the medium's subconscious mind, which would indicate that spirits are producing the phenomena after all—even though indirectly.

How about phenomena which are produced without ectoplasm? Obviously an invisible energy force is in operation and its ramifications are both startling and alarming. Soviet scientists call this force, biogravitation, which may be a basic life force that enables complex organisms to function. It also may be the material form of human mental activity. Further development will demonstrate how the mind can directly change the material world.

You will recall the message I received from Mr. Kado Dos, "Do Not Test Us, We Will Test You!" I accept the last part because there are times when I feel I am being tested—perhaps you do too! The first part of the message I believe to be a matter of interpretation; maybe we shouldn't test realities. I was a skeptic attempting to test what I thought was a hoax. It was not. I disturbed a reality and might have caused a serious injury.

In my opinion, further exploration of energies associated with psychic events will prove more important to mankind than the splitting of the atom. So go ahead and test, but be cautious, and remember—anything is possible!

Glossary

astral or etheric body—an energy body interpenetrating the physical body, which vibrates at a higher frequency than the physical body.

astral projection or OOBE (out-of-body experience)—when in sleep, trance, or during a crisis illness, the astral or secondary body detaches itself from the physical body and travels outside the periphery of the flesh. This excursion may be either conscious or unconscious.

aura—a colorful radiation surrounding the body capable of being seen by many sensitives.

automatic writing—the production of handwritten or typed messages without conscious thought from the writer.

clairvoyance—extrasensory perception of objects or of objective events.

discarnates—spirits in other states of consciousness than our own.

ectoplasm or psychic fluid—a substance that flows from the medium's body when in trance, forming into replicas of human body parts and other objects. Chemical characteristics: colorless, slightly cloudy, fluid but thready; traces of cell detritus and sputum. Deposit, whitish. Reaction, slightly alkaline.

E.S.P. (extra-sensory perception)—a capacity for apprehending occurrences without sensory contact.

exorcism—a ritual act of driving out evil spirits and demons that have possessed a human being or a physical structure.

infrared eyeglasses—used to pick up anything beyond the visible light range.

levitation—the raising of objects by supernormal means.

medium or sensitive—a psychic person through whom communication is apparently made between this world and the spirit world.

    A. **direct voice or mental medium**—discarnate voices heard through the medium's vocal cords. Written messages are also produced from discarnates.

    B. **physical mediums**—production of physical phenomena such as raps, levitation, spirit materialization, etc.

occult—hidden or concealed; beyond human understanding.

paranormal—(*para:* beyond) a force which is either paraphysical or parapsychological.

parapsychology—a field of psychology dealing with human behavior not accountable through established physical principles.

precognition—a knowledge and the prediction of future events before they occur.

PSI—a blanket name for the psychic in general. It encompasses all phenomena and experiences for which no physical cause has as yet been discovered.

telepathy—communication between the minds of two people, without the normal use of the five senses.

trance—an unconscious state in which the subconscious or psychic mind has free reign.

trumpet (seance)—an aluminum speaking trumpet used to amplify the sounds of spirit voices.

Suggested Reading List

Boss, Judy, *In Silence They Return.* Manor Books Inc., New York, N.Y., 1972.

Bro, Margueritt Harmon, *Nothing So Strange.* Harper & Row, Publishers, Inc. New York, N.Y., 1958.

Brown, Rosemary, *Unfinished Symphonies.* William Morrow & Co., New York, N.Y., 1971.

Cayce, Hugh Lynn, *Venture Inward.* Harper & Row, New York, N.Y., 1964.

Cerminara, Gina, *Many Lives, Many Loves.* William Sloane Associates, New York, N.Y., 1963.

Current, Richard N., *The Lincoln Nobody Knew.* McGraw Hill Co., New York, N.Y., 1959.

Doyle, Arthur Conan, *History of Spiritualism.* George H. Doran Co., New York, N.Y., 1926.

Feilding, Everard, *Sitting With Eusapia Palladino.* University Books, New Hyde Park, N.Y., 1963.

Fitzgerrell, J.J., *Lincoln Was A Spiritualist.* Austin Publishing Co., Los Angeles, Ca., 1924.

Grant, Joan, *Return to Elysium.* Avon Books, New York, N.Y., 1969.

Monroe, Robert A., *Journeys Out of the Body.* Anchor Books, Garden City, N.Y., 1973.

Montgomery, Ruth, *Born to Heal.* Coward, McCann & Geoghegan, New York, N.Y., 1973.

Moody, Raymond A., Jr., M.D., *Life After Life.* Mockingbird Books, Inc., Covington, Ga., 1975.

Raudive, K., *Breakthrough.* Taplinger, New York, N.Y., 1971.

Reilly, Harold J., and Brod, Ruth Hagy, *The Edgar Cayce Handbook for Health Through Drugless Therapy.* Macmillan Co., New York, N.Y., 1975.

Roberts, Jane, *Seth Speaks.* Prentice-Hall, Inc., Englewood Cliffs, N.J., 1972.

St. Clair, David, *Psychic Healers*. Doubleday & Co., Garden City, N.Y., 1974.

Sherman, Harold, *How to Know What to Believe*. Fawcett Publications, Greenwich, Conn., 1976.

Stearn, Jess, *Edgar Cayce, The Sleeping Prophet*. Doubleday & Co., Garden City, N.Y.; Bantam Books, New York, N.Y., 1968.

Sugrue, Thomas, *There Is A River*. Holt and Co., New York, N.Y., 1942.

Sylvester, Arline, *Who, Me? Yes, You*. Brandon Press, Boston, Mass., 1975.

White, Stewart Edward, *Across the Unknown*. E.P. Dutton & Co., New York, N.Y., 1939.

White, Stewart Edward, *The Betty Book*. Psychic Press, Ltd., London, England, 1970.

About The Author

Dick (R. Richard) Walker has personally made many excursions into the psychic world, but professionally he is the owner of Cheney Associates, a group of married couples who teach ballroom dancing in fraternal organizations, private clubs, and schools—and on cruise ships sailing to Australia, the Orient, Mexico, Alaska and South America.

Before entering the dance profession, in 1960, Dick was an executive in several business fields—automobile, insurance, wood products, and savings and loan. His avocation is singing. He was baritone soloist for radio station KOIN in the 1950s and also for the well-known male chorus, the Multnomah Athletic Club Balladeers, who performed with many distinguished personalities, such as Bob Hope and Bing Crosby.

Dick says, "As the son of a prominent Congregational minister who was a close friend of several college presidents, I became a college 'mongrel,' attending Willamette University, Reed College, Oberlin College and finally graduating from the University of Oregon with a B.A. degree in English literature.

"Being a P.K. (Preacher's Kid), I had two strikes against me regarding my belief in personal immortality—my father's convictions and my own rebellious nature. I rebelled against my father's religious philosophies, even though inwardly I suspected I might be in error. Finally, I decided that if there is proof that the human personality survives death, I had better find it! The evidence is rapidly accumulating and I'm discovering that, as usual, Dad was right! Much of that personal proof you will find in this book."

Dick and Dorothy Walker have two children, John and Lynn. They make their home in Portland, Oregon.